The Entrepreneur's Guidebook for Success

The Entrepreneur's Guidebook for Success

A 5-Step Lesson Plan to Create and Grow Your Own Business

Kaleil Isaza Tuzman

St. Martin's Griffin ≉ New York

www.stmartins.com

ISBN 0-312-32945-8
EAN 978-0312-32945-7

First Edition: January 2005

10 9 8 7 6 5 4 3 2 1

For my grandfather: I promise I will never forget.
And for my mother, whose midnight writing was my first
brush with entrepreneurship.

Contents

Acknowledgments   IX

Preface: Over the Andes   XI

Introduction   1

How to Use The Entrepreneur's Success Kit 2

The Components of the Kit 3

Not for the Faint of Heart 5

Chapter 1: Know Yourself   7

Discovering Your Currency 10

Exploring Your Currency(ies) 16

Getting Your Currency Right 32

Chapter 1 Conclusion 34

Chapter 2: Your Strength May Be Your Weakness   37

Self-Sabotage (Fear of Success) 38

Looking at Your Weaknesses 40

The Entrepreneur's Achilles' Heels 44

Chapter 2 Conclusion 69

Chapter 3: Believe in God but Tether Your Camel   71

Feelings and Facts 76

The Ten Most Common Areas of Observation 83

Chapter 3 Conclusion 99

Chapter 4. Beware the Butterfly Swarm   **101**

Recap 101

Step 1. Inspiration and Focus 104

Step 2. Planning 111

Step 3. Implementation and Adjustment 124

Chapter 4 Conclusion 132

Chapter 5: Enjoy the Journey   **135**

Redefining Success 136

The Power of Failure 139

The Gifts 154

Chapter 5 Conclusion 160

Acknowledgments

The idea for this kit was born when I was going through a very painful restructuring of my second business, govWorks. It became clear to me then that while there are plenty of get-rich-quick and how-I-made-a-gazillion-dollars books, there were no resources out there for the real entrepreneurial experience: the ups and downs, the struggle to find personal and professional life balance, the learning to enjoy the journey itself—with all of its unexpected twists and turns. Without having experienced that difficult time, I would not have been able to develop this kit, or understand the deeper meaning of the word "success." Therefore, I thank all the people who went through the govWorks experience with me: my business partners, investors, employees, and customers. I especially thank you because I know that, while our dreams were great, it didn't end as any of us wanted it to.

Like every entrepreneurial project, the development of this kit was truly a team effort. Samantha Ettus, my agent and dear friend, never stopped to doubt that it would happen and put the wheels in motion years ago. Susan Piver Browne helped me move from a book to a "kit" concept and introduced me to St. Martin's Press. Lisa Senz and Ethan Friedman, respectively, my publisher and editor at St. Martin's, combined three indispensable qualities: faith in the overall concept, intelligence in critiquing and modifying its contents, and patience in dealing with a first-time, fussy author. Vidushi Parmar, Rosario Davi, and Isam Walji provided essential research support, and Kristin Kimball helped me organize my thoughts well before the kit took its present form. My longtime, beloved assistant Nicole Sookdeo kept me on track and out of the office enough to finish the manuscript. Becky Rottenberg, Rachel Dodes, and Jessica Corriere provided a line of editing defense to shield St. Martin's from the worst of my errors. And Cynthia Merman, copy editor nonpareil, summed up what may have been everybody's thought at one point or another during the process: "You would be driving me crazy," she said, "if I let people drive me crazy." Thanks also to Lisa Skelton, whose careful and considerate proofreading is evident on every page of this kit.

I must also acknowledge my meditation teacher, Gurumayi Chidvilasananda, who first introduced me to the conscious path of self-discovery, without which lasting lessons aren't learned.

There were many entrepreneurs whose experiences I have learned from—and some of whose stories I have shared in this kit—to whom I owe thanks: Jason Calacanis, Marty Feinberg, Dan Hart, Joel Hyatt, Linda Rottenberg, Howard Schultz, and Charles H. Seely. There is one entrepreneur in particular who deserves special acknowledgment: Thomas J. Herman. Much of the learning reflected in this kit I owe to our struggles and successes together. I also thank the outside contributors to the Observation and Business Plan Card sections: David Camp, Alexei J. Cowett, Arnie Herz, Benjamin Dattner, Allison Dunn, Michael T. Eagan, Samantha Ettus, Joseph Hyrkin, Edward V. Mullen, Margaret Ratchford, Deborah R. Schultz, Charles H. Seely, and Dr. Andrew Zacharakis.

Ultimately, this kit would not have come together without the loving support of Catherine Wiesner, who read every line with me, stayed up every night with me, and helped me believe that I could finish on time.

Preface: Over the Andes

Many years ago, the summer after I graduated from high school, I went backpacking through Latin America with my buddy Ed. We woke before dawn one morning to fly from Colombia to Peru, to hike to the ancient ruins of Machu Picchu. We loaded our camping equipment into a small prop plane and took off with the sun. It was a clear morning, and the plane flew low. Crossing the Andes, in the gray light, we could see the dark texture of the mountains beneath us. The peaks cast heavy shadows to the  west, over boulders edged with snow and ice and sheer faces that looked as featureless as blackboards. In the valleys, it was still night. Then, suddenly, the rising sun broke over a summit and lit the valley below us. Light spread steadily over the brown-green grass of the plateaus and the black ice fields and the folds of red rock. There were no fences, no roads, no people, just great expanses of unclaimed, wild earth all the way to the horizon, where the earth curled down and away from the sky. I looked down at it from among wispy clouds, with my nose to the plane's window, mesmerized. I had seen beautiful vistas before, but this one did something to me. It made me want to yell with joy for the fact that I lived on the same planet with it. The mountains were not just big—any humble thing could be big—but imbued with *greatness*, divinity, majesty. The way I saw it, they begged for an adventure big and great enough to fill them. I promised myself then that I would do or be something that was worthy of the Andes. I wanted, in any case, to have the ambition to try.

Many years later, a lot of my dearly held beliefs about myself and about entrepreneurship have been debunked, but I have never once doubted that becoming an entrepreneur was the fulfillment of the promise I had made myself over the Andes. Being an entrepreneur—daring to try something new, anchoring an ephemeral idea to the firm soil of reality, fighting with all your strength to nurture and defend it—is a life choice that feels, to me, to be as big and as great as that Andean landscape, no matter the particular outcome.

If as you read this, there's not even a small part of you that resonates with the challenge of the Andes, then this isn't the book for you. For everyone else, Godspeed and good luck. Open to Chapter 1.

The Entrepreneur's Guidebook for Success

Introduction

If you have built castles in the air your work need not be lost; that is where they should be. Now put foundations under them.

—Henry David Thoreau

Congratulations and welcome to *The Entrepreneur's Success Kit*. This is a resource like no other. *The Entrepreneur's Guidebook for Success* that you have in front of you, together with *The Entrepreneur's Success Workbook,* the *Exercises and Visualizations* CDs, and 143 *Adviser Cards* make up a lesson plan that has the potential to change your life. You are provided with the essential tools for entrepreneurial success. Whether you already have your own business, are in the process of starting your own business, or have always dreamed of starting your own business, this kit is for you. Unlike other business books, *The Entrepreneur's Success Kit* is based on the idea that starting or running your own business is more than just a professional path—it is a *way of life*. In keeping with this unique perspective, the kit is designed to help you navigate the whole spectrum of the entrepreneurial experience, from the practical and professional to the personal and spiritual. Drawn directly from the experiences of hundreds of entrepreneurs and aspiring entrepreneurs, the resources in this kit will help you

* Identify the conscious and unconscious entrepreneurial "currencies" that drive you each and every day, from the moment you get up to the moment you go to bed at night

- Pick the right business for you

- Spot the weaknesses—your entrepreneurial "Achilles' heels"—that can trip you up along the way

- Develop a guiding business plan—whether you are still on the way to starting your business, or have been running your own company for twenty years

- Overcome obstacles in your entrepreneurial path: how to organize your time; how to develop a coherent financial model for your business; how to partner with family and friends

- Embrace your "peaks" and your "valleys," and learn to use the gifts of failure to your own advantage

- Enjoy the journey!

How to Use The Entrepreneur's Success Kit

This kit is organized as a five-part lesson plan, each part of the plan corresponding to one of the chapters of this book:

1. Know Yourself
2. Your Strength May Be Your Weakness
3. Believe in God but Tether Your Camel
4. Beware the Butterfly Swarm
5. Enjoy the Journey

Each chapter treats a different major issue, or stage, in the entrepreneurial path. Chapters 1 and 2 are more about you, the entrepreneur, addressing the process of self-discovery and assessment that all successful entrepreneurs must traverse. Chapters 3 and 4 are more about your business, covering the necessary planning and implementation that underlie every successful entrepreneurial project. Chapter 5 brings together the most enduring lessons of the entrepreneurial path: how to find peace and happiness along the way, and the real meaning of "success."

I highly recommend that you read the chapters in sequential order, whether you're still aspiring to start a business or are already well along the entrepreneurial path. Use this Guidebook as your primary guide through *The Entrepreneur's Success Kit*. As you read through the chapters in the Guidebook, you will be referred to the relevant Adviser Cards, as well as corresponding written exercises in the Workbook and specific audio tracks on the CDs. Although you can of course leaf through the Adviser Cards on your own, or pop a CD in your car stereo, what you get out of the kit will be greater in its power and effect if you start with the step-by-step lesson plan laid out in this Guidebook.

The Components of the Kit

Guidebook

This is the heart of your kit. If you follow its chapters in order, you will be guided to the appropriate written exercises in the Workbook, audio tracks on the CDs, and Adviser Cards. There are five chapters and therefore five parts to your overall lesson plan.

Workbook

This is a place for you to record your written responses to the visualization exercises and meditations that you are led through in the Guidebook and on the CDs. Your Workbook is for your eyes only, and the reflections you record in it are at times very personal.

Audio CDs

The *Exercises and Visualizations* CDs serve a dual purpose. They provide deeper, longer, and more varied versions of the visualization exercises and meditations included in the Guidebook, and they provide a form of instruction other than the written word. Both CDs are organized along the lines of the five chapters in your Guidebook. The CDs contain audio tracks that are referenced in the Guidebook and extend the lessons and visualization exercises included therein.

Adviser Cards

There are five categories of Adviser Cards in the kit, each color-coded and corresponding to one of the chapters in your overall lesson plan. Each colored section begins with a Master Intention Card, which sets the tone for the rest of the cards in the section. Each Adviser Card section also ends with a Resource Card providing useful information on additional reading material, Web sites, associations, etc.

1. Currency Cards (blue)
2. Achilles' Heels Cards (red)
3. Observation Cards (green)
4. Business Plan Cards (yellow)
5. Gifts Cards (orange)

Since the parts of the lesson plan are designed to be followed in sequential order, the Adviser Cards will be more useful if you read them in the order they are referred to in the Guidebook. However, many of the Cards also stand on their own (particularly the Observation and Business Plan Cards), so feel free to leaf through the Cards if you feel like you need a break from the structured lesson plan.

Not for the Faint of Heart . . .

The Entrepreneur's Success Kit is the first comprehensive, practical, and spiritual guide to the extraordinarily rewarding (and difficult) path called entrepreneurship. Written by entrepreneurs, for entrepreneurs, it is raw and real. Here, you will plumb the deepest valleys of entrepreneurship (from aloneness to failure and beyond) and address the most painful and personal issues (from partnership disputes to leadership transition, greed, and more). You will look at yourself in ways you never have before—buttressing your strengths and exposing your weaknesses to harsh daylight. This kit goes far beyond the usual pithy tips on how to be a good manager, or how to find the right investors for your start-up. If you're looking to really challenge yourself and erect an enduring entrepreneurial foundation—one built on self-study, humility, and discipline—then this kit is for you. But it is not for the faint of heart. Then, of course, neither is entrepreneurship. Enjoy the journey! I have, and I've made it my life's work to help others do the same.

Chapter 1: Know Yourself

Beginning the Journey the Right Way

I am often asked what makes a successful entrepreneur. Most people come into the conversation with their own answer to the question. Determination is probably the favorite, with creativity a close second. Other common answers include confidence, access to capital, education, or upbringing. More than a few chalk up successful entrepreneurship to the willingness to battle on in the face of truly insurmountable odds—you need to be a little bit *loco*, as my father would say.

In fact, after working with and listening to the stories of hundreds of entrepreneurs, I have found that there is no single attribute—whether IQ, financial acumen, or even qualities like leadership ability or stick-to-itiveness—that defines the successful entrepreneur. If there is one elixir that every entrepreneur has to drink, it is probably closer to my father's concoction of a little loco, or what my Jewish side of the family calls chutzpah. But you need even more than the mixture of courage and recklessness that defines chutzpah; you fundamentally need to *know* yourself. And this is true whatever your character and background. Recently, the Harvard Business School conducted a global survey of more than one thousand entrepreneurs from different industries, geographies, and personal backgrounds. After this exhaustive search, the one truly remarkable thing the Harvard researchers found that these entrepreneurs shared was a nearly universal emphasis on self-knowledge, on understanding what made themselves tick. In fact, when asked to explain why they chose to be an entrepreneur, more than half of the people surveyed answered that in fact they really had no choice: They knew from early on in their lives they were somehow *different* from other people and needed to follow their own path.

Does this mean that entrepreneurs are always born, not ever made? Of course not. There are guidelines for successful entrepreneurship and steps that you can proactively take to develop and enhance your entrepreneurial ability. I describe these rules and steps in later chapters. But the first step is being critically honest about one's own strengths, weaknesses, and motivations.

Talking to the Trees

David* is an entrepreneur from a tough background in rural Sullivan County, New York. I met David through an entrepreneurship retreat that I lead each year. He had dropped out of high school to tend to the financial and emotional needs of a family he and his girlfriend had started sooner than they'd planned to. Needing to support his baby daughter and her mother, David had landed the best job he could find and was soon working sixty- to seventy-hour workweeks doing tree trimming and other landscaping work on the campus of a local educational institution. But in the midst of an experience that would lead most people to despair, and with little on the horizon to make him believe things would get easier, David kept listening to an inner voice, one that he'd had since he was a kid: "What am I here to do?" he would ask himself, somehow *knowing* that his life would be different, more complete. "Why am I going through this?" Practically speaking, David was staring down the pipe of a long life of struggle and limited opportunity. But he saw the world in a different way: He believed that there was a reason, and a hidden blessing to be discovered in his current circumstances. And somewhere deep down he knew that this

*The names and identifying details of some entrepreneurs mentioned in this kit have been changed to protect their privacy.

process of discovering his own path could come only from discovering *himself*.

It happened after years of contemplation and during what at first felt like the most mundane of moments. It was a crisp October day in the Catskill Mountains, and David was up on a ladder with a clipper, tending to one of the many trees in his care. Without realizing it, he had begun to fall into the habit of quietly talking to his "patients" while doing his work—crabapples, white maples, baby birches, roses of Sharon, and fading ashes all would hear his monologue. "Just a little bit there," he would say, or, "Don't worry, I'm with you, I'm here." Though landscaping had begun many years ago for David as a default option, the only obvious job for a young, able-bodied man in a fairly desperate situation, it had become a refuge, a time when he would meditate on his and his family's future. It was especially moments like this one—high up on a ladder, all green at eye level, and all blue sky above—that David treasured and where he felt most at home. Then it hit him, "like a ton of bricks," he says now, with the benefit of hindsight and a reflective nature. "I knew then that I had *found* myself, that I was meant to start my own business and work with my 'patients' for the rest of my life. I was grateful for *everything* at that moment: the early pregnancy, my struggle to find a job and bring home enough money for my family. I wouldn't have gotten crazy and started talking to those trees—*understanding* those trees—if I hadn't been working so damn hard," he says, and now his smile broadens and his eyes sparkle, and his curving mouth seems to reach all the way to his already splayed ears, so they look like one straight line, the smile and the ears, cutting across his blond head. Today, David is the owner of one of the most sought-after landscaping businesses in New York State. David always knew he was special, and believing this, he was able to keep an open heart and mind under difficult circumstances, until his entrepreneurial adventure came to him. I don't mean to underplay all the hard work and planning that went into launching his own company (it took him almost two years just to save up and study for his first arborist exam), but David began the journey the right way: by listening to his inner voice and believing in himself.

As you read David's story, you may have said to yourself, "That doesn't apply to me." Maybe you've always known what business you wanted to launch. Maybe you think business decisions should be the product of cold calculation, not epiphanies and rhododendron bushes. Or maybe you feel you know yourself so well that you don't need to go through David's period of drift and self-questioning. The truth is that not all entrepreneurs have a stark epiphany like the one David had. But every successful entrepreneur I have ever met has, in his or her own way (and calling the process by different names), focused on self-knowledge—on undergoing a period of conscious self-questioning and self-learning. Since we live in a society that focuses on results rather than the process of obtaining those results, we don't often have the chance to see all of the millions of entrepreneurs who are out of the public eye but have achieved that magical state of knowing their underlying motivations, and balancing their economic, familial, and spiritual goals, or the early critical steps, both emotional and practical, that these people have taken to create their successes.

Discovering Your Currency

The first step in knowing yourself as an entrepreneur, and laying the groundwork for your success, is to be brutally honest with yourself about what motivates you, what I call your "currency." People are driven by different currencies: some by money, others by fame, and others by power. Still others are driven by what they perceive as the "right" thing to do, while many are motivated by an overriding desire to serve and love their family or their God. All of these are powerful, conscious motivators for human behavior. The key is to understand what really drives *you*. The better you understand your primary currency, the better you will be able to harness your energy to create and successfully launch your own business, and ultimately achieve the kind of balance in your life that will allow you to enjoy your success. For those of you who can't wait to get to the "practical stuff" (creating a business plan, hiring and firing employees, raising money, and so on), rest assured I'll get there, but without understanding your currencies first, such practicalities will be of fleeting use.

The Virgin Bastard

Richard Branson, the high-flying entrepreneur who founded the multinational Virgin Group (which includes airlines, a record label, and a retailing juggernaut), was once asked the secret of his success. "Knowing exactly what gets me up every morning," he responded. When asked, "And what would that be?" he calmly responded, "That I'm a ruthless bastard, and I'm out not to win, but to beat others into a pulp." I'm not endorsing Mr. Branson's raison d'être, nor I am condemning it, but I do admire his honesty and self-knowledge, and anybody who knows Richard Branson also knows that he was telling the truth about himself, and it's this self-knowledge that both drives his success in the business world *and* allows him to "turn it off" and enjoy giving to and loving his friends and family in a noncompetitive environment. This explains the odd combination of the Virgin Group being known for its industry-leading charitable endeavors, while its chief executive admits to wanting to rip the heads off competitors!

But, you may say, Mr. Branson's self-knowledge is unusual. People spend their whole lives trying to answer questions about their own internal drives, obsessing about subconscious insecurities and needs for "validation." Certainly, psychotherapists would be out of business without this incessant questioning. But don't let the vagueness of it all scare you away from discovering your primary currency. The level of self-knowledge that the entrepreneur needs doesn't require New Age meditation retreats or twice-a-week sessions with your therapist. It can be more basic than that. In fact, using a simple visualization exercise called *Moment of Solidity,* I have helped hundreds of entrepreneurs and aspiring entrepreneurs discover their primary currency. While this exercise may, at first, seem hokey to you, it can be of immeasurable help when approached with an open mind. I encourage you to be open.

The Progress Pose

The Progress Pose is the sitting posture that will support the visualization exercises throughout this kit. For further guidance on settling into a Progress Pose that works for you, please listen to the Progress Pose track on the first *Exercises and Visualizations* CD.

- *Sitting in a chair: Let your sitting bones press down into the seat of the chair a bit and put your feet shoulder width apart, flat on the floor.*

- *Sitting on the floor: Sit up straight—with your back supported by a wall if you need the support—with your legs crossed or in any other comfortable, firm position.*

- *Holding your Guidebook: You may hold it up with one hand, in front of your face, so you are looking straight ahead, and your neck is straight, along with the rest of your spine. If this is uncomfortable, you can gently hold it below eye level (even on your knee) and look down to read.*

You should feel powerful sitting in your Progress Pose, immovable like a rock, but with a soft foundation.

EXERCISE: *Moment of Solidity*

1. Get out your Workbook and something to write with. Put these items down next to you and find a comfortable sitting position, one where your spine is straight and elongated. Sit in the Progress Pose.

2. Let yourself move from the physical solidity and power of your current sitting posture to the more subtle foundation of your mind and the heart. Imagine yourself in the most emotionally *solid* position you've ever been in your life. (If you need to at any point, you can close your eyes, contemplate the question, and come back to this stage of the exercise when you're done.) This moment of solidity is not necessarily the moment of greatest elation in your life. Resist the temptation to think automatically of your greatest joy or achievement. Your "Moment of Solidity" may be less dramatic; it's the time when you felt the most grounded, the most together, the most in control of your destiny and at peace with your own self and your own dreams. (It could even be right now.)

3. Focus on this feeling of being rock solid in your own destiny. Don't worry if this moment doesn't come to you right away. Take as much time as you need to find this moment in your memory banks. You can close your eyes if it helps you concentrate.

4. Once you've found your greatest moment of solidity, write it down in your Workbook on pages 2 and 3. You can write in sentence fragments or shorthand that you alone will recognize. Don't worry about using proper syntax or getting the language exactly right. This is not a test, and it's for only you to read.

5. Put your Workbook down and reestablish your Progress Pose. Look *around* that moment of solidity, as if you were viewing your life on a DVD player, where you could skip to scenes before and after the scene in question. Where were you in your life at that time? What influences— people, institutions, or ideas—were most prevalent? What were you doing before and after this moment in your life? How were you spending your time every day? Try to relive that time and explore what was driving your actions and decisions at that point in your life.

6. When you are ready, open your Workbook to pages 4 and 5 and write your answers to any of the questions above. Again, don't worry about being word-perfect, but make sure that everything you write in your Workbook is directly related to that feeling of being rock *solid* in your life.

7. Turn to page 6 in your Workbook and write the following list in block letters:
> MONEY
> RECOGNITION (FAME)
> COURAGE
> VICTORY
> ACCEPTANCE
> HEALTH

8. Now comes the most critical part of the exercise. Without letting your preconceptions of what you *think* you should do affect what you *actually* do, circle the **one** word that most aptly captures your moment of greatest solidity in your life. Go with your first instinct and don't overthink it! Just circle the word that resonates most with that moment of solidity. Once you've circled it, don't change your mind. Your first instinct is almost always your best. This is your top currency, your prime motivating driver.

If you haven't done it yet, put down your Workbook now. Congratulations! Although most of us are driven by different currencies at different points in our life and career, even at different points in a given workday, it is critical to do what you've just done—identify the underlying inspiration and motivation that defines you as an entrepreneur. And getting to this primary currency can be tricky. Before moving on, let's be absolutely sure you have correctly identified your primary currency. Consider the following.

Joy vs. Solidity

Sometimes people pick their moment of greatest *joy* rather than solidity—moments like falling in love for the first time, getting married, the birth of a child, or the remission of a loved one's illness. What renders these moments of great joy less than suitable for determining your currency is that for the most part we didn't plan these events or make them happen. Most of us feel intuitively, for example, that we are not completely in control of whom we fall in love with, or whether we have a healthy baby. And although we certainly do not need to be in control of every aspect of our lives in order to be happy, the act of entrepreneurship is about creating—and being in control of—one's destiny. If, in retrospect, you feel that you may have picked your moment of greatest *joy* instead of greatest *solidity,* feel free to try the visualization exercise again.

Achievement vs. Solidity

Another approach many entrepreneurs take with this exercise is to visualize their moment of greatest *achievement* in life. Great milestones like college graduation, making partner at the firm, running a six-minute mile, or raising money for one's first business (an achievement I hope that, if you haven't already accomplished, this kit will aid you to do so soon!) often make the list. But there is a problem with visualizing your greatest achievement instead of your most *solid* moment: Entrepreneurship is not just about *doing*, it's about *being*, and every successful entrepreneur I have ever met *first* discovered a deep passion for his or her entrepreneurial path, and only later was this passion followed by outward, material success. Those entrepreneurs who identify what has motivated them in a previous achievement in life (that big promotion or buying a first home) are limiting their conceptions of what is possible—painting their future achievements, so to speak, with the brush of their previous ones. If, in retrospect, you feel that you may have picked your moment of greatest *achievement* instead of your moment of greatest *solidity*, I suggest you try the Moment of Solidity visualization exercise again.

Exploring Your Currency(ies)

Successful entrepreneurship combines both the mind (to warn you of the dangers in the path) and the heart (which will tell you to go on anyway). Having performed the Moment of Solidity exercise with hundreds of participants, I have found it is in the moment of feeling most solid in life where people are able to locate their deepest underlying motivator (what I call their currency). It is this currency, when understood and harnessed, that can carry the entrepreneur to limitless success. I have also found that of all the different possible currencies out there, most fall within the following categories:

- *Making money*
- *Achieving recognition (fame)*
- *Feeling courageous*
- *Being victorious*
- *Feeling accepted*
- *Feeling healthy and content*

Now let's take a closer look at these currencies and how they apply to the entrepreneur. I suggest that you pay close attention to the aspects of every one of the currencies because, although we all have a single predominating currency (what I call the primary currency), none of us is motivated solely by one currency. Most of us have a motivating factor that is a close second to our primary currency, a *secondary* currency, if you will. And while our primary currency tends to remain constant, our secondary currency often changes as we traverse different phases in our life or in our business's evolution. Finally, every day, we are confronted with the pros and cons of *all* the currencies listed through the ways they influence the actions and decisions of people around us—loved ones, business partners, employees, customers, vendors, or investors in our business. Therefore, I encourage you to explore all the currencies, paying special attention to your own primary currency.

Money

The easiest to grasp of the entrepreneur's currencies (and the only one that actually takes the form of currency!) is money. If you pulled the average person off the street and asked what drives the businessperson to succeed, he or she would probably tell you it's the almighty dollar. From the "Show me the money!" incantation of Cuba Gooding, Jr.'s character in *Jerry Maguire* to Yogi Berra's observation that for a ball club owner "It's not about the money, it's just about how much he can make," our culture is reared on money as the great yardstick, the measure of success in any arena. Gordon Gekko's "greed is good" mantra has never gone out of style. But there's something more to it than that. Entrepreneurs like Baron de Rothschild, John D. Rockefeller, Andrew Carnegie, and Bill Gates have always freely admitted that their personal measure of success was nothing more complex than the sheer profitability of their enterprise, and they have likewise been subject to intensive scrutiny about market collusion and competitive ethics. That said, the same robber barons above would probably also qualify as among the most generous of all time, as measured by the legacy of charitable patronage they left for the arts, education, and health care. I once heard a meditation master from India put it best: "Money is a form of energy. Like energy itself, it is neither good nor evil; only its usages can be considered such."

If the guided exercise above yielded money as your primary currency, consider yourself lucky. First of all, you are in the minority (most entrepreneurs, when they're honest with themselves, are driven by the more ethereal currencies of feeling courageous, victorious, accepted, etc.). Secondly, you now have a clear set of criteria with which to make decisions about which business to start, which employee to retain, which vacation to take. Indeed, you have a single criterion: How will this decision impact your bottom line? Knowing that you are primarily motivated by wealth creation will crystallize many of the tough decisions I address in the upcoming chapters and make your entrepreneurial path easier in many respects. A big downside, however, is that being an entrepreneur is probably the toughest way to make a living! It reminds me of Jack Welch's commencement speech some years ago at Harvard Business School. "What I really wanted to do when I was young was be an entrepreneur, open a restaurant," he began. "But then I realized it's easier to run a Fortune 500 company." If you are an entrepreneur who values the currency of money over all others, you may want to focus your efforts on a business in a field like retail, affinity marketing, investment banking, or outsource manufacturing.

More on Money Currency

The additional resources in this kit will alert you to things to watch out for if money is your primary currency, including positive aspects like your capacity for single-minded focus and negative aspects like your tendency to lose sight of long-term objectives in favor of short-term profits. See Currency Cards 1-4 to further explore the strengths and weaknesses of money as a primary currency, including more about which businesses you might be best suited for and which you might want to stay away from; complementary secondary currency matches; reading list recommendations; and famous money currency holders. You can also follow the audio tracks on the money currency on the *Exercises and Visualizations* CDs.

Recognition (Fame)

After money comes what I call the "denial" currencies: recognition, courage, victory, and acceptance. Though some people have hang-ups about admitting their devotion to the almighty dollar, fewer people admit to yearning for fame, or for the feeling of being courageous or victorious, much less working to feel "accepted." Nevertheless, it is my experience that these are the emotions that drive most entrepreneurs, and it's best to come to grips with these motivating principles so as to harness their formidable power.

Recognition, or fame, is perhaps the most basic of these currencies. Entrepreneurs may shy away from admitting it openly but, after all, who doesn't want to be famous? The explosion of reality TV around the world and the cult of Internet entrepreneurship in the late 1990s are symptoms of a similar strain in our global society: linking visibility with success. In a perverse way, even the terrible terrorist acts of recent years are part of this ceaseless struggle to be "seen" on the global stage. While entrepreneurs like Mark Cuban (owner of the Dallas Mavericks and founder of Broadcast.com) and Oprah Winfrey have managed to successfully use their self-admitted desire for fame and visibility as the fuel in their entrepreneurial quest, many entrepreneurs suppress and deny their desire for recognition. When this happens, it creates a highly corrosive influence, sneaking its way into your life and work decisions without your realizing it. Every time you are bombarded with a late-night TV or radio advertisement with someone hawking his or her wares, you can be sure that there is an entrepreneur who is torn between wanting to be in business and wanting to be a celebrity.

I have battled with this demon myself, allowing a documentary film crew to follow the development of one of my previous businesses, govWorks, ostensibly in the development of a video case study for a business school. In fact, I secretly wanted the

More on Recognition Currency

The additional resources in this kit will alert you to things to watch out for if recognition is your primary currency, including positive aspects like your charisma and leadership ability and negative aspects like your tendency to ignore the less "glamorous" aspects of business—developing your product, customer service, financial management, and so on. Consult Currency Cards 5–8 to further explore the strengths and weaknesses of recognition as a primary currency, including which businesses you might be best suited for and which you might want to stay away from; complementary secondary currency matches; reading list recommendations; and famous recognition currency holders. You can also follow the audio tracks on the recognition currency on the *Exercises and Visualizations* CDs.

world to see me as I "heroically" built the company, and when the documentarians finally made the footage into a feature film that was seen by millions of people, I achieved that secret desire. As a result of being caught up in the visibility of the movie and other high-flying aspects of govWorks (including going to fancy industry conferences and getting to meet the president of the United States), I didn't attend to my underlying enterprise as I should have—to my clients, vendors, and employees—and my long-term business prospects suffered. I realize now that the company's problems stemmed from my own failure to understand and control my currency of recognition. The key with the currency is to harness its power; if you are an entrepreneur who values this currency above all others, go into a field where visibility and notoriety are usually intrinsic goods, like entertainment, novelty products, even politics!

Courage

I am repeatedly surprised and moved by the degree to which courage (or to be more precise, the feeling of being courageous) motivates so many entrepreneurs. For many years I was embarrassed by my practice as a small child to pray for an "adventurous life." At bedtime, when the rest of our family was saying nightly prayers for things like world peace and getting up again in the morning after laying oneself down to rest, I would mutter things like, "God, please don't make my life boring," or "God, I want to be a hero." For many years I thought I was different and strange—that is, until I found out how many other entrepreneurs uttered similar prayers in their past. When I give a seminar for current and aspiring entrepreneurs and we go through the Moment of Solidity visualization exercise you just performed, more than half consistently associate the word "courage" with the time in their life when they felt the most solid.

More on Courage Currency

The additional resources in this kit will alert you to things to watch out for if courage is your primary currency, including positive aspects like your relentless optimism and your ability to truly innovate, and negative aspects like your tendency toward a crusading mentality that can cut you off from needed feedback or lead you to become unduly fascinated with innovation for its own sake or the conceptual "newness" of an untapped market. Consult Currency Cards 9–11 to further explore the strengths and weaknesses of courage as a primary currency, including which businesses you might be best suited for and which you might want to stay away from; complementary secondary currency matches; reading list recommendations; and famous courage currency holders. You can also follow the "courage currency" audio track on the *Exercises and Visualizations* CDs.

Courage can be a great and a pure motivator. Entrepreneurs who are self-aware enough to identify the feeling of living a courageous (and risk-taking) life as their primary currency are also more likely to avoid that danger zone where pride comes before a fall. You may know what I mean: Look at your own life and think about the subtle difference between taking a courageous stand on something (like starting your own business or respectfully disagreeing with your boss) and pride or hubris (like trying to be the hero and do a project all on your own, or refusing to ask for directions). When Teddy Roosevelt, an oft-quoted master of entrepreneurial thought, was just getting the building of one of the great entrepreneurial projects of all time, the Panama Canal, under way, he was being grilled by the national press on the truly massive investment that the canal would require. "Why are you doing this?" he was asked aggressively at the contemporary equivalent of a modern-day press conference. "Because I am afraid to," the president of the United States responded.

As entrepreneurs, when, like Roosevelt, we are conscious of the battle with our own fears, we can literally move mountains. Courage can be the greatest currency of all for the entrepreneur, as long as the battle for courageous action is waged internally and does not become hubris and the search for vainglory. If courage is your primary currency, a classic entrepreneurial start-up may be right for you, including research and development–rich projects involving things like consumer products, health care, technology, and communications.

Victory

This is Richard Branson's currency—his desire to "beat others into a pulp." Despite the occasional Richard Branson out there, victory, or the desire to win, pure and simple, is perhaps the rarest yet most often caricatured of the entrepreneur's currencies. While many might think that this currency encompasses the basic competitive nature of anyone venturing into a new marketplace or starting a new business, the raw desire to win is rarely sustaining enough for the long-distance race that is entrepreneurial life. As any marathon runner (or any great athlete, for that matter) will tell you, the true competition is really with *yourself*, not with others in the race. While individual TBS executives may have been driven by their competition with old network standards like NBC and CBS, in building his start-up television network, Ted Turner was driven by his desire to simply be the best he could possibly be, not the fact that he was breaking the oligopoly of the market's major players.

A recent University of Virginia study explored the competitiveness of entrepreneurs versus nonentrepreneurial business decisionmakers and found that the entrepreneurs were more than twice as likely to collaborate with their competitors (on broad areas such as research and development, production, and sales and marketing). In other words, while entrepreneurs are often portrayed as being cutthroat competitors, they are actually much more likely to cooperate with each other in the marketplace. As with all the entrepreneurial currencies, the key to successfully harnessing the desire for victory is understanding its hold on you.

If you are like most entrepreneurs and are instinctively a team player within a community of peers (i.e., other entrepreneurs), you should search out opportunities for cooperation in the start-up phase and beyond, through organizations like the American Chambers of Commerce, the Young Entrepreneurs' Organization,

More on Victory Currency

The additional resources in this kit will alert you to things to watch out for if victory is your primary currency, including positive aspects like your capacity for laserlike focus and attention to detail on certain projects and negative aspects like your tendency to become obsessed with your entrepreneurial mission and lose perspective surrounding personal relationships and family life. Consult Currency Cards 12–15 to further explore the strengths and weaknesses of victory as a primary currency, including which businesses you might be best suited for and which you might want to stay away from; complementary secondary currency matches; reading list recommendations; and famous victory currency holders. You can also follow the "victory currency" audio track on the *Exercises and Visualizations* CDs.

state-level economic development agencies, and the Small Business Administration.

If you are like Richard Branson, however, be honest with yourself about it up front. You may be better off picking up on an existing idea in the marketplace (rather than coming up with the "next big thing"), where you are fueled by the fire of your competition and the prospect of your executing on the idea better than everyone else. For those victory-driven entrepreneurs who do have an instinct toward collaboration in the market, highly competitive areas that also benefit from concentrated supply chain cooperation—like manufacturing, transportation, and financial services—may be the right choice. For the Richard Branson types, the bruising competition of areas like retail, telecommunications, or publishing might be more appropriate fields of endeavor.

Acceptance

Certainly the most Freudian of the entrepreneur's currencies (implying secret insecurities and feelings of deficiency), acceptance is a powerful force that can be insidious if allowed to run unchecked in our lives. Every psychotherapist worth his or her salt will tell you that our behavior is unconsciously driven by our insecurities. If we are afraid of being thought of as dumb, for example, we may compensate by getting additional degrees or professional certifications, or by choosing a career path that is traditionally thought of as intellectually challenging. If we are instinctively anti-social and scared of others, we may compensate by being as hip as can be, like the jet-setting protagonist in Carly Simon's "You're So Vain." There are students of entrepreneurship who view many individual entrepreneurs' decisions to start their own businesses and sometimes take outsized risks as an unconscious compensation for having been made to feel like an outsider as a child.

They believe that these entrepreneurs must show that they can succeed by their own rules in order to become accepted in a world that rejected them as a child. There are many adherents to this school of thought, and I have been witness to the large number of entrepreneurs who associate the word "acceptance" with their visualization of the most rock-solid moment in their life. Of course, "acceptance" is a multifaceted word. It can refer to being accepted by others—almost like getting a coveted pass to an exclusive club—or it can refer to the entrepreneur's understanding of the need to integrate into his or her surroundings and circumstances without unnecessarily "rocking the boat."

Dina DuBlon, the CFO of JPMorgan Chase and one of corporate America's most senior women executives, embodies the act of blazing an entrepreneurial path within large organizations, having aggressively worked herself up through the ranks of the banking industry over thirty years. When Dina, a friend and a mentor of mine, started at Chemical Banking Corp. in the early 1970s, she was the only woman in a class of more than seventy management trainees. When I asked her at a lunch a couple of years ago what she thought had made her successful in her career, the answer I got was a complete surprise. "I have learned," she said, leaning forward with a fork in hand, "to refrain from saying everything I think." While a cynic might say that's the epitome of the big-company, bureaucratic survival strategy—or worse, an example of a chauvinistic attitude toward women in the workplace—Dina looked at the issue in an entirely different way: She knew what her eventual goal was and understood the power of the currency of acceptance—that a certain degree of conformity would balance her edge and boldness, and help her achieve her end. Entrepreneurs are not always firebrands or "market disruptors," as certain business-school professors label them. They can also be quiet and method-

More on Acceptance Currency

The additional resources in this kit will alert you to things to watch out for if acceptance is your primary currency, including positive aspects like the team-oriented approach that allows you to conduct the "orchestra" of your business, and negative aspects like the occasional paralysis you experience when it comes to making the tough decisions in your business—decisions that by definition involve trade-offs, hurting some people and benefiting others. Consult Currency Cards 16–18 to further explore the strengths and weaknesses of acceptance as a primary currency, including which businesses you might be best suited for and which you might want to stay away from; complementary secondary currency matches; reading list recommendations; and famous acceptance currency holders. You can also follow the "acceptance currency" audio track on the *Exercises and Visualizations* CDs.

ical, understanding their surroundings and building business relationships over decades, or introducing slight improvements into already efficient and robust marketplaces. In these instances, the currency of acceptance (or social, market, and economic validation) is of the highest order. If this is your primary currency as an entrepreneur, areas like distribution, human resources training, claims processing, or other supply-chain oriented businesses may be right for you.

Health

Health is the one currency that people who have not gone through the Moment of Solidity exercise generally respond to with "huh?" or "how can health be an underlying motivator for something as proactive as entrepreneurship?" Well, the word "health" here has layered meanings. When people visualize their moment of greatest solidity in life, one of the more common memories conjured up is that of coming out of a period of physical, emotional, or psychological discontent and pain. "Health" in this context is really a synonym for "contentedness" or "without pain." And as an Epicurean will tell you, the meaning of life for many of us is the escape from pain. It is no surprise, then, that entrepreneurs of all types (prototypical small-business owners and individual proprietors, entrepreneurial actors within large organizations, writers, designers, artists, etc.) describe their entrepreneurship as their life-sustaining force. For some, life can be so painful that their most salient entrepreneurial currency is the constant effort to escape from certain aspects of reality. By way of example, most people aren't shocked to hear that Virginia Woolf turned to writing "to escape the pain of my days," but are surprised to hear that Steve Jobs returned to run Apple for a similar reason: "Because if I hadn't, I would have gone crazy."

While this currency can be the most uncomfortable to speak

More on Health Currency

People sometimes confuse the currency of acceptance (a desire to be validated, in a sense, loved) with that of health (a desire to be at peace and without suffering). In fact, they are very different. The additional resources in this kit will help you separate these motivational strands and alert you to things to watch out for if health is your primary currency, including positive aspects like the mind/body/spirit balance that enables you to take in stride the bumps and bruises of the entrepreneurial life, and negative aspects like a tendency toward complacency around market shifts and encroaching competi-  tion—sometimes until it is too late to make necessary changes in your business. Consult Currency Cards 19–21 to further explore the strengths and weaknesses of health as a primary currency, includ- ing which businesses you might be best suited for and which you might want to stay away from; com- plementary secondary currency matches; reading list recommen- dations; and famous health cur- rency holders. You can also follow the "health crisis" audio track on the *Exercises and Visualizations* CDs.

about, it *is* real and prevalent, and its power can be harnessed only by looking it in the eye. If your primary currency is health—as a conscious effort to escape physical or emotional pain or, less dramatically, simply a desire to feel balanced and at peace in your life—entrepreneurial projects that are very interpersonally oriented, hands-on, and creative are likely to be best for you. These include the healing arts, of course, but also graphic design, freelance copywriting, photography, management consulting, and the educational fields.

Getting Your Currency Right

Having reviewed the six entrepreneurial currencies of money, recognition, courage, victory, acceptance, and health, resist the temptation to cast out of hand those you don't think apply to *you* (although you may see how they apply to others). A professor of mine used to call this tendency of mixing up what applies to us and what applies to other people "attribution distortion."

Attribution distortion can be problematic for entrepreneurs trying to get to know themselves better and identify their primary currency. We must all get into the habit of seeing things as they *are*, not as we would like them to be. That's why I used the Moment of Solidity visualization exercise instead of asking you outright which of the six currencies you think applies best to you. In a sense, it was with the idea of catching you unawares, with less attribution distortion risk. As entrepreneurs (really, as people), most of us are in chronic denial about what really drives us and who we are: It's as if we look in the mirror but see someone else staring back. Richard Branson, who knows he is driven by the fierceness of battle and the thrill of victory, is a rare breed. Most entrepreneurs who are driven by fame will tell you (if they haven't found their moment of solidity) that they are driven by courage. Entrepreneurs who are

Attribution Distortion

Psychologists have shown that if you present someone with the same failure (getting lost on the way to a meeting, for example, or submitting a work product late) in her own experience and in the experience of someone else, the person you ask almost always attributes the other person's failure to his incompetence (he didn't read the directions carefully enough; he procrastinated on the work report). Meanwhile, the same failure in the experience of the person you ask almost always is attributed not to her own incompetence but to the surrounding *context* that was out of her control (the directions weren't written down well; she wasn't given enough direction from higher-ups on the work assignment).

Similarly, the distortion exists when people assess reasons for success. The person you ask sees her success (hitting a baseball, for example, or impressing a colleague) as a function of her own competence or ability rather than as a function of her surrounding context (an easy pitch down the middle; a dim-witted colleague who is easily impressed). Because as entrepreneurs we are riding hard the waves of success and failure, we must be particularly vigilant about attribution distortion and careful not to dismiss others for their failure or give ourselves too much credit for our successes. Humility (especially in the search for self-knowledge) is key.

driven by acceptance may try to tell you (and, more importantly, themselves) that they are driven by money.

The key to navigating the waters of self-discovery is being honest and flexible with yourself in the process. The truth is that most of us are driven by different currencies at different times in our lives and careers. And even those currencies that seem the most remote to us are in fact close by and critical for us to understand—by dint of being the primary currency for our biggest customer, our business partner, or even our loved one. Most of us have secondary currencies—what in Eastern philosophy are sometimes called "ascendant" tendencies—that may not be what drive us to get up and go to work every morning but that are strong motivators that arise—for better or for worse—at the critical moments in our life. Although courage is my primary currency, I am often struck by the almost magnetic sway of my desire for recognition that, if not understood and controlled, can sometimes stir me to do pretty stupid things. Winston Churchill (whose primary currency was probably victory) was self-aware enough to know about his secondary currency of acceptance. "I am generally effective," he said, "except on those days when I am keen to be liked."

Chapter 1 Conclusion

Getting to know ourselves is not always a pleasant affair. We must look both our strengths and shortcomings squarely in the eye. The currencies in this chapter are neither good nor evil. They each have pros and cons that can work to either stabilize or undermine the aspiring entrepreneur. By making the commitment to understand these motivational currencies, and to get to know yourself better, you have begun the entrepreneurial journey the right way.

Before moving on to the next chapter, go over the Moment of Solidity exercise as many times as you need to. Beware of attribution distortion; strip away the layers of preconceptions about yourself and get to your motivational *essence*, however unexpected or unpleasant. Don't stop there: Go back and study all the different currencies, for they hold sway over your entrepreneurial experience at different times and in different ways—sometimes even through other people. The blue Currency Cards and the audio exercises on the CDs that correspond to this chapter will help you delve deeper into the different currencies and the concrete ways they can affect your business life, positively and negatively. They will also prepare you for the next chapter in the lesson plan, "Your Strength May Be Your Weakness." In Chapter 2, I look more closely at the common pitfalls on the entrepreneurial path—what I call the entrepreneurial Achilles' heels.

Chapter 2: Your Strength May Be Your Weakness
Overcoming Your Achilles' Heels

In Chapter 1, I explored the currencies of entrepreneurship, those underlying motivators that drive you on your path to create and to live your business life outside of the average bounds. Your entrepreneurial currencies are at least as important as the nature of the actual business you are venturing to launch. Whether you run a five-person flower shop or a hundred-person aircraft parts distribution business, your success or failure will be determined more by your ability to bring your outer activities and your inner currencies into alignment than by those things that are, in the end, outside of your control—foreign competition, for example, or changing consumer behavior.

Focus on Yourself

I was once at a weekend-long business retreat with Joel Hyatt, professor of entrepreneurship at the Stanford Graduate School of Business and the founder of Hyatt Legal Services. Exasperated after my third round of questions on the characteristics of the legal services marketplace when he founded his revolutionary "legal insurance plan" product, he finally burst out, "I don't know! Once I do my research, I start focusing on me and my team and *stop* focusing on the stuff I can't control anyway." Joel, a lawyer by training, was always an entrepreneur at heart. His currency is courage, and he traffics in its close cousin: innovation.

By truly *knowing* yourself, you maximize your chances to channel your abilities and ambitions toward the appropriate type of business for you in the long term. You also minimize the chances that your preconceptions of the type of business in which you *should* be involved will intrude and dictate the type of business in which you *actually* become involved. You must be wary of the self-destructive tendencies that we all share—the voice that says "You're not good enough," or "You can't succeed in *that* area." Knowing your powerful underlying currency—wealth, contentedness, or the feeling of being courageous—acts against self-doubt and self-imposed limitations. Self-knowledge is a weapon against all the voices (outside and within you) that say "You can't."

Self-Sabotage (Fear of Success)

In this chapter, I unmask the surreptitious enemy of every entrepreneur. You're probably asking, "What would that be? Lack of start-up capital? A paucity of emotional support from family and friends? Faulty or absent advance planning and budgeting?" Although these are all real obstacles for even the most seasoned business manager (and I address them in the chapters to come), *self-sabotage* is the true bête noire of the entrepreneur. You know what I am talking about. Self-sabotage is the little gremlin we all carry within. It is the "reset" button that sometimes goes off in our life, putting an abrupt end to a particularly beautiful adventure—a relationship that brings us uncomfortably close to our heart's innermost recesses, or a job that affords us the opportunity finally to work on what we've always said we wanted to do. And then something just "goes wrong."

Self-sabotage is perverse. It strikes us just as we are approaching the summit of our aspirations, as if there were some abstract moral arbiter deciding we don't *deserve* it. These steps backward are seemingly against our will and out of our control—the result of an insurmountable behavioral quirk in our business partner, for example, or an irreversible change in our employer's corporate priorities that kills our pet project. But beware! These events, seemingly so out of our control, are actually perfectly in line with our subconscious desire to put the brakes on—lest we actually manage to reach our utmost goals and then find ourselves asking, "Now what?" Most of us are deathly afraid, deep down, of actually achieving our dreams. We have tied happiness so firmly to some far-off goal that we are mortified by the possibility that we won't actually be happy once we notch that first (or hundredth) million, publish that first (or tenth) book, or marry that first (or third) Mr. or Ms. Right. Fear of failure? "Forget about it," in the words of Coach Bear Bryant. "It's the fear of success that paralyzes most of 'em."

We must learn to release ourselves from this fear of success. If there is anything we as entrepreneurs know deep down, it is that *we* create the reality around us. It's this knowledge that makes us "different," in the words of the Harvard Business School study. The entrepreneur knows—*you* know—that there are no excuses in life. And although we intuitively grasp the idea that we manifest our own destiny, we as entrepreneurs are paradoxically the biggest victims of self-sabotage. Since we have the chutzpah to follow our dreams and to risk failure and humiliation in the world's eyes, we are forced to face the demon of self-sabotage at a higher level. We have a potentially disastrous Achilles' heel: The same power of creativity and determination that allows us to start a business from scratch, to give form to the formless, also allows us to clearly visualize the pitfalls down the road and almost manifest our falling into them. Saint Augustine called this the "visionary's paradox." As if testing God or fate, as entrepreneurs we give ourselves permission to skate close to the edge, so to speak—and sometimes we stretch the healthy risk taking of entrepreneurship into the taking of unnecessary risks, and embark on knowingly fruitless adventures. In my lecturing and consulting with entrepreneurs from around the globe, I am continually astounded by entrepreneurs' ability to *ignore* their own inner voice and creatively bring about their own downfall. Like gamblers who can't stop playing for the big score, even the greatest entrepreneurs wrestle with this tendency toward self-sabotage. "My biggest risk?" intoned Jimmy Goldsmith, a self-made (and self-aware) billionaire and one of the great business innovators of the late twentieth century: "Myself."

Looking at Your Weaknesses

In Chapter 1, you used the Moment of Solidity visualization exercise to discover your primary entrepreneurial currency. In this chapter, you will again go through a visualization exercise, this time as a means to discover your entrepreneurial Achilles' heels—the particular traps of self-sabotage to which you are individually prone. Though this may at first seem like focusing on the negative, I have found in my work with entrepreneurs that—being generally self-confident and optimistic—they need to spend more time analyzing their weaknesses than their strengths. And to compound the problem, entrepreneurs have overactive minds and rarely stop to reflect or examine ourselves. After years of working with entrepreneurs to successfully grow their businesses—and examine their tendencies toward self-sabotage along the way—I've discovered that it's very difficult to teach most entrepreneurs; the best you can do is help them to teach themselves. Hence the visualization and self-discovery technique I am using with you here. Now, let's focus on uncovering and slaying the demons of self-sabotage. I call this next visualization exercise the Hanuman Stance.

A Good Kind of Hurt

One student in a seminar I gave in Indianapolis several years ago put it this way: "Thank you for helping me teach myself this class," he said, having initially been very resistant to some of the exercises, especially those that dealt with the Achilles' heels. "It was a good kind of hurt." He was forty-six years old, recently divorced, admittedly "stuck in his ways," yet on the verge of starting a new business. Today, he's the CEO of a $22 million maintenance services company and is in the process of merging his company with one of the largest players in his industry. If he can do it, so can you.

Why Hanuman?

Why was this exercise called the "Hanuman Stance"? Hanuman is a mythological being, with the body of a man and the head of a monkey, who comes from the Ramayana, an ancient Hindu text. Hanuman is the servant of Rama, one of the many demihuman manifestations of God in Hindu mythology. He is always depicted with a chiseled, musclebound frame and a large, bejeweled mace in his right hand. He is the ultimate warrior of justice, abhorring violence but eradicating the demons of this earth at his master Rama's command. But what is most impressive about Hanuman is not his superhuman strength or acts of courage on the battlefield. It is Hanuman's consummate devotion to his master's command and his immovable faith that give him his unique place in the pantheon of legendary warriors. When ordered to find something just underneath the waves, he swims to the bottom of the ocean in search of his objective. When he cannot retrieve a particular healing herb for Rama, he brings back to him the whole mountain that is its habitat. Hanuman blends deific strength with humility and a no-excuses "task" orientation, as a business-school professor might call it. He embodies the opposite of what

EXERCISE: *The Hanuman Stance*

1. Find a quiet and private place. Have next to you the Workbook and a writing utensil. Again, take up the Progress Pose used in the Moment of Solidity exercise (described on page 12). This strong yet comfortable pose, of elongated spine and relaxed, stable sitting bones, is the foundation for all the visualization exercises in this kit.

2. Take a few deep breaths. Start to imagine the strongest-looking statue of a standing figure you have ever seen. The muscles are rippling, the stance is confident and limber, with the weight shifted a bit to one leg. Perhaps there's a mace (a spiked club) in one hand of the statuesque figure, or a broadsword. This figure, determined yet at peace with itself, is the epitome of confidence, power, and righteous service to a higher good—the righter of wrongs, the avenger of ills, and the distributor of justice. It is the kind of figure that takes your breath away for an instant when you first gaze eyes upon it. You instinctively inhale a deep breath, all the way down to your diaphragm, and without putting words to why or how, you feel inspired, knowing at some deeper level than you did a moment before that you *can* conquer the world—that you *can* be a great and good parent, businessperson, partner, lover, warrior, servant.

3. Now let that feeling of greatness permeate your being. Continue to breathe deeply, all the while gazing up at this statue of chiseled power. As you breathe, let each inhale give life to the figure in front of you. Let each exhale entail a lifting of the great mace in this warrior's hand, with the attendant movements of the body to support the mace's anticipated striking. If it helps, you can imagine the warrior in battle, bathed in light, lifting up the mace to strike down the enemy.

4. Look upon the demons of self-sabotage that came to mind reading the last section. As you breathe out, let the mace come down on your shadow enemies. Let it crush your fears, your insecurities, your worries. Let the mace strike and let fly the gremlins that haunt your entrepreneurial endeavors—all the obstacles, excuses, doubts, fears, and "I can'ts" that you have unconsciously and unwittingly invited to your entrepreneurial table. Call them out as the mace strikes them down. These gremlins stand no chance against the mace of the warrior. They are meek, pathetic, small, petty. Breathe slowly and with strength, letting the mace do its work, disbursing the gremlins, striking and disbursing again if one attempts to return.

5. And as you purge them, give names to the enemies. Do it. Don't stop and think. You know their names. Call them out loud. As the mace flies, say them louder. You can repeat the same one as many times as it needs to be thrashed. Be as broad or as specific as comes to you naturally. Don't self-censor. "Doubt!" may be one, or "Fear!" Others might be more specific: "Business plan still unfinished!" "Can't find the time to work on my entrepreneurial project!" or "I'm out of money!" Shout them out! "I don't finish what I start! I don't have what it takes to run my own business!" Wham! The mace puts an end to that. Knock as many of these fears and obstacles as you need to. Breathe powerfully all the while. Be strong. If you want, close your eyes and come back to the text later, as you knock them away. Keep going until there are no more enemies left.

6. As your environment begins to calm down and you have shouted out all your fears and doubts, let the warrior begin to rest. Let yourself come to repose. Begin to breathe more slowly. You have done your job. You are at peace. You can relax.

7. Take up your Workbook and turn to page 40. While this visualization exercise is still fresh in your mind, write down all the different gremlins you exorcised with your mace. Don't censor yourself. You don't have to share this with anyone. Just write *all* the gremlins you can remember, even those that sound silly to you now, a few minutes later. Jot them down as quickly as you can remember, in shorthand if need be. It's okay to add others that you didn't think of during the visualization exercise, but don't overintellectualize the process (for example, don't let "I can't get start-up financing" become "I am having difficulty generating a value proposition that is compelling enough for an angel investor"). Although you may not see it right now, the page where you have written these fears, doubts, and obstacles has taken on an important place in your entrepreneurial evolution. By committing to paper these elements of self-sabotage, you have taken away some of their power over you. They are nothing more than items to be crossed out now, gremlins to be decimated by your inner warrior.

my father used to call the "average attitude." As a child, if I were looking in vain for a lost toy, he would say, "You're looking for it and praying to God you don't find it." This is the attitude of most people when pursuing their dreams and objectives.

From the first time I led entrepreneurs in the warrior visualization exercise, Hanuman was the figure that came to my mind. As an entrepreneur, we need to be Hanuman, and we need our powers of mind, body, and spirit to be Hanu*men* and Hanu*women* at our disposal. We must have unflagging faith in the face of seemingly impossible situations. Howard Schultz, the founder of Starbucks, said it best: "If people thought it was possible before, someone would have done it already." Especially when we take on the warrior stance and set about to slay the demons of our doubts and fears, we must make our mind and body a consummate servant of our will—à la Hanuman, who was willing to swim to the bottom of the ocean on a command.

The Entrepreneur's Achilles' Heels

If you want to compare and contrast the results of your Hanuman Stance exercise with some of the common gremlins encountered by other entrepreneurs, you can turn to the Achilles' Heels Cards that go with this chapter. These cards are tied to the themes elaborated in the rest of this chapter, and will provide you some counsel on how to overcome common entrepreneurial obstacles—practical and emotional—and get information on other problem-solving resources on these subjects. The red Intention Card and the Chapter 2 CD audio tracks on the Hanuman Stance are good tools to come back to whenever you are feeling overwhelmed; they will help you stay focused on overcoming the obstacles in the entrepreneurial path that you recorded in your Workbook.

After having gone through the Hanuman Stance exercise with entrepreneurs of many varied perspectives and nationalities, I am always reminded of how much all of us in the global community of entrepreneurship have in common. Below, I distill the major issues that regularly come up in response to the Hanuman Stance exercise. As you read through the following entrepreneurs' Achilles' heels, think about how these match your own gremlins that you articulated in your Workbook.

The Money Trap

The definition of this one may surprise you. No, I am not talking about the stylized view of the corrupting influence of wealth expressed by many of our society's liberal or religious commentators. I don't think money automatically "corrupts." Nor do I think greed is the downfall of our moral character. Properly focused, the pursuit of wealth can lend the kind of clarity to business and interpersonal interactions that allows for healthy relationships to flourish. As I said before in the discussion of money as a primary currency, money in and of itself is neither good nor evil; its use can be either. I think entrepreneurs actually have a healthier relationship with money than almost anyone else because they know that it doesn't grow on trees. Most entrepreneurs are deeply grateful for whatever wealth they have accumulated. Most have traversed very lean times and know how thin the line really is between financial success and failure. While the Ivy League–educated investment banker might unconsciously look down on the construction worker and the messenger, wondering why they "chose" their paths in life or didn't "apply" themselves more, the entrepreneur knows that launching a successful business is at best three parts hard work and four parts luck and that we're all only "one step away from the shoeshine."

The entrepreneur's "money trap" I am talking about here is something I also call the "if-only" disease. As entrepreneurs, we sometimes get too fixated on the need for financial capital. I can't tell you how many entrepreneurs I have worked with over the years who start our working sessions by saying something akin to, "If I had the money, I would . . ." And they apply it to absolutely everything:

If I had the money, I would hire a crackerjack salesperson.

If I had the money, I would pay off the bank and be able to open up new stores.

If I had the money, I'd be able to buy out my partner and stop having the business dragged down by our quarrels.

If I had the money, I would be able to get more inventory and grow myself out of this mess.

If I had the money, I'd be able to show my vendors we're solvent and improve financing terms.

While all these statements undoubtedly feel very true for the entrepreneur uttering them at the time, the "If I had the money" pretext is a trap. It serves to insulate us from really dealing with our problems. Anytime we can't figure out a solution to a particular entrepreneurial challenge, we can just say "If I had the money . . ." Money, after all, solves everything. Now, I am an entrepreneur as well, and if you are sitting there thinking, "But if I had the capital, I really could [fill in the blank]," I empathize with you. Boy, do I empathize. The reason I have listed the money trap as the first entrepreneurial Achilles' heel is that I know for a fact it is the most insidious, the most difficult to get across to thick-headed entre-preneurs, and the most difficult to conquer. No matter how many times you read this kit, no matter how many times you hear one successful entrepreneur (a Michael Dell, for example, or a Marty Schottenstein) tell you that he made it because he *didn't* have access to capital in the beginning, you will have trouble believing what I have to say here: Money is *not* the answer to your entre-preneurial snags.

My Own Money Trap

Years ago, when I was CEO of a government contracting firm, I was involved in the development of a joint case study on public sector entre-preneurship for the Wharton School of Business and the University of Pennsylvania Ronald S. Lauder School of Government. I had the good for-tune to interview a number of entrepreneurs in the budding "electronic government" marketplace—the area that would eventually include elec-tronic and online processing of things like parking tickets, tax payments, fishing licenses, and beach permits. It was a fascinating group of people. There were some who had recently left government service after having served for decades as county commissioners, municipal treasurers, or chief information officers for cities. Others were venture capital–backed young bucks, with terrific ideas for making government work more effi-ciently and for "bankable" technology. Still others were traditional tech-nology consulting firms that were moving from private sector work in their local communities to the idea of providing similar services to their local government bureaucracies.

Tracking all of these entrepreneurs closely over the last five years (I still speak with many of them monthly or quarterly), I have been struck by an irre-ducible lesson: Without exception, the more bootstrapped the project and the less well capitalized, the more successful it ended up being. The companies that succeeded in this market are those that, instead of raising a lot of money and building products to meet a customer's needs *tomorrow,* developed *with* their customers' buying patterns, taking it slow if need be, and having patience. In fact, those companies that had their wish early on—that pos-sessed the capital required to hire more salespeople, build out product capa-bility, etc.—are not around anymore. I should know: Mine was one of them!

If you can learn to escape the money trap early on in your entrepreneurial career, you will be blessed with a rare, innate advantage. Therefore, when you lack the capital that you view as the key to a particularly problematic lock in your business, practice the ability to view this problem as an *opportunity*. Let's practice this now.

EXERCISE: *The Money Trap*

1. Find a quiet place to sit, take a few deep breaths, and take as long as you need to assume your Progress Pose. Have your Workbook ready.

2. As your breathing slows and your mind becomes more still, ask yourself, "What would I do if I had more money for my business or business idea?" Once again, don't censor your responses—censure and the stifling of free thought and creativity are banes of entrepreneurship. The ideas that come to mind might be grand ("I would change the way people think about physical fitness"); they might be basic and tactical ("I would hire a salesperson in Wichita"); or they might be somewhere in between ("I would pay a designer to work with me on the new clothing line"). Whatever your responses are, let them flow. You may want to close your eyes while you imagine all the possibilities.

3. After you have thought about these what-if-I-had-the-money scenarios for a few minutes, perhaps with your eyes closed, turn to the money trap section on page 43 of your Workbook. Write down the top three things you'd do with your business or your business idea *if* you had the money. You can include as much detail as you feel comfortable with. For example, while you might have said to yourself, "I would open a store," feel free to tighten up the thought and actually brainstorm a bit on location, staffing, etc.

4. Now, take the three things you'd do if you had the money and let them "rest" in your mind. Let them percolate there in your brain like a pickle in brine. You might imagine them more concretely, or you might begin to poke logistical holes in your original idea. Either way, get more and more excited about accomplishing your if-I-had-the-money wish list and visualize the actions coming to fruition. You have opened that new store, hired that new assistant!

5. As you think about the three actions on your wish list, slowly begin to "take away" the money. Literally, imagine removing dollars from the situation. If you were envisioning adding some products to your shelves, imagine accomplishing the same thing . . . but this time *without* any money to purchase the new products. If you were imagining using the funds to safely leave your workaday job and finally launch your brilliant business idea, now imagine doing all that exciting stuff . . . only *without* the money. The key is to continue visualizing the outcome of your actions as actually happening; it is only the outside capital that has disappeared. Does this seem preposterous to you? How can you be expected to visualize investments in your business and then visualize those investments with no money? It doesn't work that way, you might say. Well, I have news for you: It *does* work that way. There are always alternatives to cash money when assembling the resources to build a business. There are other entrepreneurs and more developed businesses that will take a flyer on you and extend you some working capital or human resources to develop an idea or a product—perhaps for a share of future revenues. There are always talented salespeople out there who will take a risk on you as an entrepreneur and accept a commission-only type pay package for a short period of time, and so on.

6. In the next section in your Workbook, write the ways that you could make your top three wish list goals happen without outside money. Think of people you can go to, businesses you can partner with, skills and services you can barter with. Be creative and don't be embarrassed about the constraints on your resources.

Lack of capital can enforce discipline. If you don't have the money to hire a new salesperson, it may force you to come up with a purely incentive-driven compensation plan that is ultimately better for your business, or even force you to find an employee elsewhere in your business who should be let go or reassigned to sales duties. Lack of outside capital can also deepen and strengthen your customer relationships. One of the most commendable solutions to a need for investment capital in developing a new product, for example, is to partner with an existing or prospective client for that product who will bear some of the financing cost in its development because he or she has a vested interest in seeing you ultimately deliver it to the market. As perverse as it might seem, even at the very incipient stages of your entrepreneurial project, you can be grateful for your lack of start-up capital. I know dozens of entrepreneurs who look back and give thanks that they didn't have the money to jump too hastily into their chosen project. The sometimes painful wait and endless grubbing for start-up capital affords you the opportunity to think through your project more carefully and—if you're open to it—get the feedback of many knowledgeable and insightful people along the way.

The Funky Office and the Millionaire

I had dinner recently with a seasoned (he'd blanch if I called him "elderly") entrepreneur named Marty. When I met him at his office, I was struck by the humility of his surroundings. I knew him to be a terrifically successful businessperson—one of the creators of the media barter business in the United States—and yet his office was accessed by a rickety old elevator, and the carpets and couches in the anteroom looked like they hadn't been replaced since the Carter administration. Finally, after having a meal with him at one of New York City's finest eateries and seeing his apartment full of Impressionist paintings worth many millions of dollars, I couldn't hold back my desire to understand the paradox. "Marty," I started, nervous he would take it the wrong way, "your office is so . . . funky . . . and yet you have such beautiful taste—" He cut me off. "Kaleil," he said, leaning forward with the persona of a loving old Jewish uncle dancing perceptibly behind his stern expression, "in business, you must always tell yourself you have nothing in order to get something." Marty may take this lesson to an extreme, but you will be much better served erring toward his perspective in your entrepreneurial adventures than whining to yourself about the "if-onlys" that would come with more capital—that is, succumbing to the money trap.

Ultimately, the money trap is a form of self-sabotage; it is an inner gremlin making an excuse, inventing an obstacle that prevents your full self-realization and success. As you go through this kit, find appropriate moments to refer back to your "if-only" wish list you wrote earlier. These are your excuses, the goals you have set up in your own mind as being unachievable today. They represent the ways you've fallen into the money trap. Achilles' Heel Cards 1–2 will give you more tips on the noncash resources you can access as an entrepreneur in any market. The audio tracks on the *Exercises and Visualizations* CDs entitled "Chapter 2: Avoiding the Money Trap" will help you move away from "if-only" consciousness (and don't fret, in the next chapter I explore how to successfully *raise* money for your start-up venture).

The Worthiness Trap

In the second—and perhaps deadliest—of entrepreneurial Achilles' heels, we come head-to-head with every businessperson's worst enemy: self-doubt. It is critical to distinguish between the appropriate, healthy dose of fear and nervousness that is shared by every entrepreneur when setting out on a risky project and the demon of self-doubt that tells the entrepreneur that he or she can't succeed, or doesn't *deserve* to succeed. The latter is by far the more insidious of the two forms of self-doubt and leads to what I call the worthiness trap. Entrepreneurs tend to be good at overcoming their fear of jumping off the diving board, even if it takes lots of time and great effort. Although the voices of self-doubt are ever present (even for the seemingly supremely confident Oprah Winfreys of this world), the entrepreneur *feels* that he or she is different and can usually power through the mundane concerns of risk of failure or humiliation. More complex and difficult to handle is the inner self-sabotageur that tells us, "You are not worthy," stopping us in our tracks just as we are at the cusp of success.

The worthiness trap is uncomfortable for many people to read or even to think about. "I am not like that," is what we'd all like to think. We are confident. We believe in ourselves. All this worthiness stuff sounds like psychological mumbo-jumbo, anyway. Ah, would that it were true. Away from the office, away from your business partner or your newest client, go deep down and be completely honest with yourself. How often do you unconsciously sabotage yourself—showing up late to that critical meeting, not responding to that client proposal because "you probably wouldn't win it anyway," or dropping the ball on a potentially key business contact because you secretly feel he or she is out of your league? These are the real-life moments of every entrepreneur. We cripple ourselves with self-doubt every day, sometimes in overt but mostly in subtle ways. It is the voice of self-doubt that causes the procrastinator to put off that critical work, for fear of not being able to produce the quality product he'd like to when he finally puts his mind to it. It is the voice of self-doubt that inhibits the business manager from taking that leadership course that would help her improve her relationship with her employees—for fear of not being capable of following the course's directives. It is the voice of self-doubt that prevents many would-be entrepreneurs from launching their businesses in the first place.

This is not to imply that entrepreneurs should not have fear. Fear is natural and healthy. I have often functioned as a panelist in so-called business plan competitions, where gutsy aspiring entrepreneurs present their business ideas to a panel of judges, often for the prospect of start-up financing. Whether in London, England; Punta del Este, Uruguay; or Palo Alto, California, the presenting entrepreneurs exhibit the same mixture of exhilaration and fear. While I consider myself a fairly easygoing judge, some of my peers relish ripping apart the business plans in front of them. I have observed that the winning participants in such contests do not get selected from the small pool of those who stride in full of confidence and fearlessness, but are from those who acknowledge the holes in their plan, the inherent risks and dangers in their forward path—those who exude a subtler kind of confidence, the belief in their own ability to confront, deal with, and learn from the inevitable bumps and bruises they will sustain. Though they are as subject to fear and nervousness as the next person, they do not let the fear paralyze them and, most important, by knowing themselves they have come closer to slaying the demon of self-doubt.

I was a baseball pitcher in college, and my coach called this principle of success by another name. "Make them beat you," he would say on his frequent visits to the pitcher's mound, when I had lost my control. "Don't beat yourself. Throw them the ball so they can hit it." This is a critical lesson for entrepreneurs: Facing the prospect of losing is part of the game. Just don't beat yourself. You are worthy of success. Get out there and make the market— not yourself—prove you wrong.

EXERCISE: *The Worthiness Trap*

Use the Chapter 2 audio track on the *Exercises and Visualizations* CDs corresponding to "The Worthiness Trap" as a guide for the exercise below and to help you adopt techniques for recognizing your own worthiness.

1. Open your Workbook to page 46 on the worthiness trap. As you did with the money trap, find your Progress Pose. Breathe deeply.

2. Without censoring yourself, write down all the ways that self-doubt manifests in your entrepreneurial project/business.

> **3.** After you've given yourself time to reflect, go on to page 48 in your Workbook and write down the things you can do to eliminate these episodes of self-doubt. These may be as simple as "go for a run and get my juices going" or as seemingly complex as "dissect the root causes of the self-doubt and see if I can identify the difference between well-placed concern about lack of preparation and misplaced fear of the unknown."

For additional guidance on how to avoid the worthiness trap and help in identifying specific symptoms of self-doubt's sometimes sneaky infiltration of your business life, look at Achilles' Heel Cards 3–5 on *Slaying Self-Doubt*.

The Forgetfulness (Self-Delusion) Trap

There is a story about a spiritual seeker who went to a great master to inquire about how his life had gone astray. He had been a respected monk of another order but had fallen from grace and was now considered an apostate by his community. "I cannot find God in the ways of a monk, nor can I find God in the ways of the world," complained the frustrated seeker, imploring the master for help. "You have already found everything you are looking for," said the master. "You have only forgotten."

It is so easy to forget. As children, we enjoyed the mere texture of each experience—the passing scenery of a simple car ride, the unique facial expressions of a new acquaintance. But as we got older, we became inured to things. The fascination with newness faded, and we forgot the magic in the simple things in life. On an only slightly more complex level, the same thing happens in business. We forget what used to make us excited to get up in the morning; we forget the pure enjoyment of landing a new client, having a profitable month, or coming up with an innovation in our product. Most important, we forget our moorings, what our underlying currency is. When we forget what drives us, we forget who we really are, and we begin to become deluded. It is in this danger zone that we fail to control the negative tendencies that accompany our respective currencies and are subject to their dark sides. In this state of forgetfulness, we become unbalanced, and our currency can lead us astray.

Stakeholders

"Stakeholder" is an old word for people who hold bets. Today it also refers to the community of individuals that make up the entrepreneur's world. It comes from the idea of being accountable to your *share*holders when you are managing the development of a business. But entrepreneurs are responsible, in a sense, for many more people than the shareholders—or investors—in their business. They are also accountable to employees, partners (individuals or other companies), customers, vendors, lenders, even their own family who supports them—emotionally or financially— through their daily grind. All of these people (as well as investors, or shareholders) make up the stakeholders of the entrepreneurial enterprise.

- The currency of money can lead to short-term greed at the cost of long-term customer, employee, or vendor (collectively, stakeholder) relationships.
- The currency of recognition can lead to egotism and self-aggrandizement that is off-putting to stakeholders.
- The currency of courage can lead to the assumption of excessive risk.

- The currency of victory can lead to an obsession with performance *relative* to others instead of absolute results.
- The currency of acceptance can lead to business decisions that overly value stakeholder comfort and put your business at long-term risk.
- The currency of health can lead to laziness.

"We have met the enemy and he is us," the comic book protagonist Pogo said. We are our own worst enemy when we forget our true nature. We drift from our core values and, before we know it, we are in a hole too deep to get out of. I have been there myself. One of the businesses I started ultimately went into Chapter 11 bankruptcy, in large part due to the fact that I couldn't handle *success.* As we added clients and our staff grew to more than three hundred, I thought we were invincible. The currencies that had gotten me there—courage and recognition—turned on me and morphed into unnecessary derring-do and egotism. I lost my moorings. I learned about the forgetfulness trap (and the money trap) the hard way. I hope you don't have to. I am always surprised by the preponderance of entrepreneurs going through bankruptcy and restructuring who attribute their predicament to this same disease: forgetfulness. Although they use slightly different words to describe it, the themes are universal: forgetting what got them there and losing their moorings. For some entrepreneurs, this means not working as hard as they used to; for others, it means losing touch with the original customer base and not hearing customer feedback. For me, it meant losing the discipline concerning investments and expenditures that I had exhibited in my first venture.

It all goes back to our initial lesson in this kit: *knowing yourself.* The only thing worse than not knowing yourself to begin with is forgetting who you really are along the way. It is like forgetting how to drive a car: You are much better off losing control of the vehicle as you try to pull out of the driveway at five miles per hour than at seventy miles per hour on the highway. The same is true of entrepreneurial endeavor. Once you are out on the highway, with your business humming along, you are in control of a much more powerful—and potentially destructive—vehicle. It is in this later zone that you still hold the power of your intentions and past successes but with the danger of your present self-delusion. Your daily decisions are not just your own anymore; they now affect the lives of all of your stakeholders. Without necessarily being aware of it, you are at that point probably the role model for other people—both close family members and observers from afar whom you will never meet. You hold a certain power in your hand. It is a bit like being given a sacred mission. You have been entrusted with something beautiful, and you must be ever watchful of the very human tendency to *forget*—to forget your currencies and the qualities of your deepest self. It is in this danger zone where accidents happen.

The very troubling thing about forgetfulness and self-delusion is that they are difficult to self-diagnose. By definition, self-deluded entrepreneurs don't know they're not on the right path. They simply think they have "grown" or "changed" in ways that have expanded their skills and capabilities. Self-deluded entrepreneurs may trick you with their impenetrable confidence and savoir faire. They may appear as if they're on top of the world . . . right before the fall. But there are ways to diagnose self-delusion, including the application of special scrutiny to dramatic changes in relationships with family and friends. And there are ways to guard against it, by identifying at least one or two people around you who can and will give you critical feedback fearlessly. Clues to potential entrepreneurial self-delusion include dramatic changes in products or services that an early-stage company offers, the type of client that a company serves, or the financing/growth strategy of a start-up company. Although we tend to attribute these changes to "personal growth" or some sort of great epiphany (and indeed there are times when, as entrepreneurs, we legitimately have positive and sudden business breakthroughs), it is best to dig deeper, because dramatic shifts of these types are often symptomatic of our straying from understanding our primary currency and the results of self-delusion.

EXERCISE: *The Forgetfulness Trap*

Use the audio track on the *Exercises and Visualizations* CDs corresponding to Chapter 2, "The Forgetfulness Trap," as a guide for the exercise below and to help you adopt techniques for the very challenging task of identifying—in effect, *remembering*—your own forgetfulness.

1. Open your Workbook to page 49 and take as much time as you need to find your Progress Pose. Breathe deeply.

2. Without censoring yourself, write down the top three areas in your entrepreneurial project/business in which you may have strayed from acknowledging and balancing your primary currency and demonstrated forgetfulness in your relationship with yourself. Of all the exercises in this kit, this one may require the greatest level of honesty with yourself. (If you have trouble with this self-diagnosis of forgetfulness when simply following the written word here, listen carefully to the audio track.)

3. As you have done previously, take a short break, then write in the next section of your Workbook the steps you can take to "rediscover" your core principles and avoid the forgetfulness trap.

I will discuss the nettlesome reality of strategic business shifts and changes in the next entrepreneurial Achilles' heel, the holding-on trap. But first, Achilles' Heel Cards 6–7 will provide you with additional tools to identify self-delusion, stay true to yourself and your currency(ies), and avoid the forgetfulness trap.

The Holding-on Trap

The holding-on trap flows from the forgetfulness trap. To the extent that we forget what really drives us and who we really are, we also begin to delude ourselves into thinking that we are someone we're not. That is to say, we think we can be everything we need to be for every stage of our business's evolution. As I discuss in Chapter 4, entrepreneurs tend to overestimate the need for major changes in strategy and market approach. Because the creative explosion of the start-up business is so powerful and emotive, as entrepreneurs we often think a business's development must always be this chemically reactive, so to speak, and ever changing. In reality, an entrepreneurial project goes through different stages, but the most successful endeavors prefer the "slow-and-steady" method of evolution over the "rocket ship" or "race car" approach. In their seminal book *Built to Last*, James C. Collins and Jerry I. Porras likened the start-up business's journey to a great mountain climb and identified that the most durable and successful businesses experience plateaus, or pausing points, in the climb. While the organization rests and consolidates at each plateau, there is often a handoff between the leader of the previous stage in the climb and the leader for the next stage. Most students of entrepreneurship have come to the conclusion that these handoffs are more critical to a business's successful evolution than the brilliance of its original idea, the stamina of the founder, or the market forces that have enveloped its growth.

The very premise of the handoff accepts the idea that we are each driven by our own underlying currencies and that we must know ourselves to be successful. What Collins and Porras and other scholars have concluded is that just as we each have our own underlying currencies, we also each have "core competencies" that flow from these underlying drives. I may be extraordinarily talented at getting people to believe in a revolutionary business idea, for example, but extraordinarily inept at organizing a hiring plan and product development plan that will turn this idea into a reality. It is this implicit division of labor that many entrepreneurs intuitively acknowledge when they go into business with friends and partners who have complementary, and totally different, skills. Think Bill Gates, the software visionary, and Steve Ballmer, the operations chief. Or Howard Schultz, the coffee guru, and Orin Smith, who helped Starbucks grow from a good idea and two stores in Seattle to more than seven thousand stores and a global brand nonpareil. In each business I have started, I have sought a complementary partner, someone who brought a key element to the table that I clearly didn't. We tend to think of our complement in terms of particular business competencies (for example, when I started a software company, I had an idea of how the product would work, but if I hadn't partnered with a software engineer, I never would have gotten it off the ground). Finding a complementary *personality* is often even more important than finding someone with complementary business *skills*. I couldn't have successfully launched any of the three businesses I co-founded without the challenging, and sometimes sparring, voice of my business partners. In each case, their engineer- and accountantlike attention to planning and detail kept in check the dreamer in me which, left unchecked, could get us off track and ahead of ourselves. To this day, when I take on a new interim CEO assignment (as part of my current business,

Recognition Group, working with entrepreneurs and small companies), I bring with me a COO-like partner, a mooring influence who will make sure my grand plans get translated into concrete products and financial spreadsheets. At the same time, my perennial optimism is an essential ingredient to a venture's success, particularly in some of the turnaround situations that we get involved with. In sum, it takes a combination of different types of skills *and* personalities to make an entrepreneurial project work.

The holding-on trap occurs when entrepreneurs believe that they can be all things to their business at all times. This is the entrepreneurs' tendency to try to do everything themselves. It is characterized by an inability to differentiate the truly important tasks from the mundane ones. The entrepreneur in the holding-on trap cannot delegate and burns out. Or he or she grows a business to twenty people and three stores, only to become stuck for years and not know how to grow more. (The twenty-person mark is a rough level of employees at which experts have observed that new management skills of delegation, worker monitoring, and quality control are needed to further develop a business.) The holding-on trap can completely debilitate the entrepreneur, leading even to hopelessness and depression. More often than not, when I meet an entrepreneur who describes himself or herself as feeling frustrated, stagnated, or overwhelmed, the real problem is the inability to recognize where he or she needs to hand off certain responsibilities in the business to others.

There are many simple solutions to the holding-on trap. In today's economy, there are a panoply of choices in business outsourcing that entrepreneurs can turn to for those tasks requiring skills they lack, from administrative services like 401(k) management or payroll administration to outsourcing of sales force functions to human resources training. The simplest solution to the holding-on trap is to develop a strong team of people around you as an entrepreneur. If you're the owner of a one-person business, this means you too! For one-person operations, it means the development of a close circle of advisers (friends and business associates) who have skill sets different from your own, add different perspectives, and aren't afraid to speak their mind. We often forget that the primary reason why corporate boards of directors exist is not just to approve things like stock option plans and rubber-stamp financial reports, but also to give the business manager critical feedback and advice. The start-up entrepreneur rarely has a traditional board of directors, so it is especially important to seek out complementary—but not necessarily complimentary!—points of view. Paul O'Neill, the former U.S. Treasury secretary and well-respected CEO of Alcoa, probably said it best, in answer to the proverbial what-has-made-you-successful question: "A phobia of yes-men," he answered quietly and confidently. It takes a truly self-aware entrepreneur to seek out the company of those who consistently challenge him or her, but this is the secret to avoiding the holding-on trap. Whether you are actually handing off your company's CEO role to someone else, or simply handing off the handling of a particular client pitch, you've got to be disciplined about recognizing your strengths and sticking to your core competencies as much as possible.

EXERCISE: *The Holding-on Trap*

Use the track on the *Exercises and Visualizations* CDs corresponding to Chapter 2, "The Holding-on Trap," as a guide for the exercise below and to help you address techniques for identifying where you are having trouble handing off responsibility and moving to the next level in your business.

1. Open your Workbook to page 52 and take as much time as you need to find your Progress Pose. Breathe deeply.

2. Without self-censoring yourself, write down the top three areas in which you are overstretching your natural abilities in your entrepreneurial project/business and suffering from your inability to hand off responsibility or internalize outside counsel.

3. Take a short break, then write on page 54 of your Workbook ways you can free up responsibility and get beyond feeling "stuck." Think about tasks you can delegate to team members or partners (and about any extra guidance they might need to be empowered for delegation to work). List aspects of your day that could be made more efficient by letting go of your need to do everything and control everything.

For more advice on how to identify your hand-off plateaus in your business's evolutionary climb, and ways to avoid this trap, see Achilles' Heel Cards 8–10.

The Expediency Trap

The last of the traps of self-sabotage, the entrepreneurial Achilles' heels, could also be called the laziness trap. This trap is more about moral laxness than physical torpor. In the context of the forgetfulness trap, you saw how the path of entrepreneurship is akin to driving a car at high speeds, its highs and lows accentuated by the perils and the weight of responsibility for your company's stakeholders. In the same sense, entrepreneurship is a perilous crucible for moral discovery, where the boundaries of ethics and propriety are constantly tested. This should come as no surprise, given that entrepreneurial endeavors by definition test the outer limits of a market's possibility—in consumer tastes, business process, technological innovation, and other areas. It is no accident that the entrepreneurial adventures of late nineteenth-century characters like Andrew Carnegie, John D. Rockefeller, and J. P. Morgan pushed much of our current antitrust legislation into existence, or that the excesses of the late '90s Internet and telecommunications boom led to various restrictions on stock market and investment practices. On the level of national actors, the untamed entrepreneurial energy of upstarts like the United States, Japan, and China over the last 150 years has pushed rules of fair trade, intellectual property protection, antidumping, and other so-called best practices into the lexicon of international economics. Entrepreneurship is the jagged edge where capitalism's farthest reaches are explored. And every system, as the philosopher John Rawls would say, is defined by its extremes.

The expediency trap comes into play when entrepreneurs flag in their vigilance. Entrepreneurs must always be attuned to their role as moral exemplars. As they jostle for market share, and battle competitors, they must always be aware that they will be under more scrutiny than the established enterprise. Credibility is the entrepreneur's most coveted—and elusive—possession. And while our society publicly trumpets its devotion to the entrepreneurial work ethic and American individualism, in our daily choices—what we buy, whom we listen to, how we think—we are nevertheless drawn to the establishment: that which is safe and tested. We instinctively shy away from new things. Years ago, an economist at the University of Chicago conducted a study of individual purchasing patterns in an office environment. He found that mid-level, white-collar employees of a large company were almost seven times more likely to purchase a piece of branded merchandise (like an Izod shirt, a cup of Starbucks coffee, or a Nissan) if they had seen the same brand of merchandise consumed by one of their peers at the office. You are probably nodding right now. The fact of the matter is that you don't need somebody like me to tell you that human beings feel safety in numbers and act like lemmings. In fact, your recognizing this reality is what makes you an entrepreneur in the first place, at least in part. However, what most entrepreneurs fail to grasp is the implication that this aspect of human behavior holds for their own success or failure.

At a certain level, the masses, so to speak, want new products and business initiatives to fail. The media, the retail distribution network, even your office cubicle neighbor are constantly watching for failings in the entrepreneur and his or her products and services. Any cutting of corners, any act of expediency over attentiveness to detail—whether in product construction, hiring practices, marketing partner selection, or any other decision—can be the death knell of the entrepreneur. Have you ever considered why certain brands go from being "chic" to "cheap"? Why new eateries go from "in" to "out"? We are a culture of fads, and one of the entrepreneur's greatest challenges is to avoid becoming a fad. Favoring expediency over quality, or what is easy over what is right, is the quickest path to "faddom" and failure. In her recent book *Brand New: How Entrepreneurs Earned Consumers' Respect from Wedgwood to Dell*, Nancy Koehn, professor of marketing at Harvard Business School, profiles six of the world's top brands, and observes that every single one of them labored in relative obscurity for decades. She also observed that the companies behind these brands almost all shared a primordial commitment to the highest ethical standards in their business practices, long before corporate mission statements and PR spinmeisters came into vogue.

As entrepreneurs, we must resist the temptation to do everything fast. This requires some unlearning for many of us, since we are often drawn to the speed and spontaneity of the entrepreneurial life. I am reminded of one of Tom Wolfe's "Masters of the Universe" in *Bonfire of the Vanities*. "Tomorrow?" he asks. "Tomorrow's always too late for me." But the long-term success of an entrepreneurial venture is founded on a consistent, enduring commitment to quality and the highest ethical standards. This means that things sometimes take longer than we would like and cost more than we anticipated. While immediate gratification is often the entrepreneur's addiction, discipline and absolute moral rectitude are a must for long-term successful entrepreneurship and the only way to avoid the expediency trap.

The Expediency Trap: Karen's Story

We've all suffered the consequences of eating too much after a period of fasting or skipping a meal. Similarly, the cash-starved entrepreneur too often takes in too much capital (equity investment or some sort of loan) when it suddenly becomes available.

This tendency to gorge oneself is one of the most common manifestations of the expediency trap, and it is not limited to taking in too much investment capital. Entrepreneurs succumb to the same impulse when accepting more client work than they can reliably handle, or growing the team of employees more quickly than they can effectively manage.

It takes a very strong internal compass to avoid the expediency trap. Karen, a past client of mine, was the head of a supply-chain management consulting firm that focused on helping big consumer products, pharmaceutical, energy, and manufacturing companies save money on purchasing orders. She had founded the company about seven years before hiring my firm, during which time she had lived through booms and busts in her industry. During the late '90s in particular, Karen had received numerous offers from venture capital firms to provide financing to transform Karen's company from what they considered a "boring" consulting firm (Karen had grown her company to "only" ninety or so employees in her first four years in business—a number people saw as low in those heady days) into an "exciting" *software*-focused services firm. It was hard to argue with the logic at the time: It felt like a "presto-changeo" world, where you mixed a little bit of capital (say, a few million dollars!), threw in a fledgling business and a business plan with the word "software" or "Internet" in it, and—lo and behold— you'd be a billionaire. In reality, though, this was not a model to develop a real business but a half-baked scheme to bet on the IPO market.

But Karen stuck to her guns. While other small consultancies that were also started in the mid-90s were taking in lots of venture capital or getting absorbed by high-flying Internet firms, Karen decided to continue along the slow-and-steady route. She determined that her clients, always her number one priority (and several of which were Fortune 100 companies that had taken a flyer on her when she had gone out on her own years ago), looked to her business for unbiased, focused services and expertise. By building a software product, she would stretch herself beyond her natural skill set and lose her objectivity when it came to recommending technology purchases to clients.

Though some employees and service providers made fun of Karen for her "backwardness," her decision to avoid the boom market incentives of 1997–2000 in fact positioned her for long-term success. As the recession hit in 2001, and the capital markets virtually shut down, her competitors' multi-million-dollar expansion plans and dependence on outside money led many of them to bankruptcy. Those that did make it through were bruised and battered, and Karen's clients remembered her dedication to principled and unbiased service in the face of temptation. No one wanted to do business with companies that might disappear or change tack completely tomorrow, and Karen found herself with many new clients and sustained positive cash flow. In early 2004, I helped Karen sell her business for a very nice sum.

EXERCISE: *The Expediency Trap*

Use the track on the *Exercises and Visualizations* CDs corresponding to Chapter 2, "The Expediency Trap," as a guide for the exercise below and to help you address techniques for identifying places in your entrepreneurial life where what is expedient might be winning out over what is *right*.

1. Open your Workbook to page 55 and take as much time as you need to find your Progress Pose. Breathe deeply.

2. Without censoring yourself, write down the areas in your entrepreneurial project/business where expediency has prevailed in tough decisions, or where you have strayed from your ethical moorings. This is a difficult area in which to be honest with yourself, and it can be painful to confront. This makes it all the more important that you record and diagnose these moments of frailty. Remember, all the materials in your kit are private and for your consumption only.

3. Take a short break, then write on page 57 of your Workbook people and activities in your life that keep you tied to your "moorings"— ethical, religious, quality control, or even customer service oriented.

Achilles' Heel Cards 11–13 will help you avoid the pitfalls of the expediency trap and give you some practical tips for protecting against taking shortcuts in your business.

Chapter 2 Conclusion

In the Chapter 1 lesson plan on "Knowing Yourself," you explored your underlying currencies and started your entrepreneurial journey in the right way. In the Chapter 2 lesson plan on "Your Strength May Be Your Weakness," you have been exploring the gremlins of self-sabotage that can surface in your entrepreneurial endeavors. Although it may be painful at times, it is critical to face your weaknesses and potential pitfalls as an entrepreneur as early and as candidly as possible. Now that you have thoroughly explored the five self-sabotaging Achilles' heels of entrepreneurship—the money trap, the worthiness trap, the forgetfulness trap, the holding-on trap, and the expediency trap—I encourage you to spend time going over the Achilles' Heels Cards and *Exercises and Visualizations* CD tracks for each trap described in this chapter. These will help you to further diagnose which of these areas of potential self-sabotage may be manifesting in your professional life, and apply remedies to help you combat these tendencies. The Intention Card for this chapter will help you stay focused on the warrior within and practice eradicating the demons of self-sabotage.

Now that you are equipped with the necessary self-knowledge around your own entrepreneurial currencies and Achilles' heels, you are prepared to delve into the more practical elements of entrepreneurial project development. In Chapter 3, I explore how to lay the practical foundations that will channel your innate entrepreneurial qualities into a structured and successful enterprise.

Chapter 3: Believe in God but Tether Your Camel
Practical Lessons for Successful Entrepreneurship

Congratulations! You have made it through the New Agey introspective stuff. Now you're probably thinking, "When do I get to the practical advice?" Well, it's forthwith, as my lawyer likes to say. The key is to remember that, without an understanding of your underlying currencies, and without a watchfulness for your Achilles' heels of self-sabotage, the practical stuff won't do you much good. Without the deeper knowledge of your own tendencies, strengths, and weaknesses, your mind will be like a sieve: No matter how many times you fill it up with practical tips on how to raise money or launch your first product, the lessons will quickly dissipate. At the same time, it is possible to err in the other direction. An exclusive focus on the metaphysical aspects of entrepreneurship—passion, drive, faith, and perseverance—will not work either. Entrepreneurial success is not solely a function of things like inspiration, strength of conviction, or even self-knowledge; it is these things, *plus* detailed planning, attention to detail, and the flexibility to constantly learn and make adjustments that produces a lasting entrepreneurial endeavor. A story from the ancient Sufi tradition illustrates this paradox:

The Servant and the Camel

A wealthy man and his servant were making their way by camel across a featureless desert. They traveled hard through the shifting sand dunes, and by afternoon they had drunk the last of their water. The camel was thirsty and irritated. The servant, who had never been so far from his home village, imagined that they were lost and would soon die an ugly death, crawling over the dunes toward mirages. He began to panic. The master, a religious man, told him to pull himself together and to trust in Allah.

That evening, they reached a lush oasis. The servant rejoiced. He watered the camel and drank deeply from the sweet water, and praised Allah for his guiding hand. The master went to bed, reminding the servant of his duty to stake and tether the camel. But the servant, who was elated with God's compassion, was also hungry and exhausted, so he ate some dates and fell into a deep sleep. When the sun came up, the camel was gone.

"What happened? I told you to tether the camel!" the master said.

The befuddled servant said, "But you taught me to trust in Allah, so before I went to sleep I asked Allah to take care of the camel."

The master said, "Let me rephrase that lesson: Trust in Allah, but tether your camel first."

When I launched my first business, I trusted completely in the inevitability of my own success. I was on fire with inspiration, and I rode the momentum that came from it. Faith, inspiration, and momentum are the essential ingredients of any entrepreneurial venture, and without them, you're sunk. But when you're full of so much good energy, it's tempting to let a lot of important camels wander untethered into the desert. I trusted and believed so strongly in our idea that I failed to nail down key agreements, make some tough (and controversial) decisions, and prepare backup plans. What I'm saying, fellow entrepreneurs, is that when entrepreneurial ecstasy rubs up against business requirements, extra vigilance is required, from day one. In my first business, it was especially those tasks that were emotionally difficult or ran counter to the bright enthusiasm I was feeling that slipped through the cracks.

In this chapter, you are going to learn to tether your camel. I start with a visualization exercise, with the intent of helping you identify where, in your current start-up business (or even your current business *idea*), you are leaving camels untethered and perhaps avoiding making necessary but difficult decisions. In the sessions I lead with entrepreneurs, it is consistently this exercise where the most breakthroughs of understanding take place.

EXERCISE: *The Observer*

1. Assume your solid but relaxed Progress Pose once again. (You may prefer to have your eyes closed and follow this exercise through the *Exercises and Visualizations* CD track corresponding to Chapter 3, "The Observer.") If it helps you maintain your posture, you can lift the Guidebook in front of you, so that you are keeping a straight back and neck.

2. Now you are going to practice *observing*. Begin to observe your life at this moment. Resist the temptation to pass judgment or make any decisions about whether what you see is right or wrong. Just observe. Observe your stress level, your strained relationships with certain partners or loved ones, your frustration at not moving forward with a plan you told yourself months ago you would embark on, or the fact that you didn't write that business plan yet or aren't sticking to that exercise regimen as you promised yourself you would. Observe, as if you were a plane or a bird flying over your own life, calmly viewing all there is to see. Also observe the wonderful elements of your life: your small acts of courage, the things you do each day that perhaps no one else sees, the feeling of love and security that overcomes you sometimes when you see your child running in the yard, even the curvature of the neck and the rise of the cheekbone of your loved one. Observe how you feel on a beautiful sunny day, when you wake up well rested. Observe.

3. Turn your observation to your entrepreneurial project. Observe the ways you are telling yourself you can't move forward ("I don't have the time," for example, or "It's too much risk," even "I'm too old to be doing this"). Observe these excuses. Now observe the blessings and opportunities your new business or business idea brings, or will bring, to you. Observe the satisfied customer. Observe how happy you are delivering another beautifully cared for product to a client, or even just making payroll for another month! Observe the potential for self-fulfillment and groundedness from your new business project.

4. As you observe, fly lower to the ground, so that you begin to observe the little things in your day: the way you are keeping your accounting records, the attitude you display with your regular clients, your partners, and your employees.

5. If you have not taken the leap to start your own business, observe your daily life just the same. Keep flying lower and lower, until you are actually observing the most minute level of detail: the clothes you're wearing, or what you choose to eat for lunch. Again, no judgments allowed (resist the urge to criticize the stain on your shirt, or your tendency to resort to quickie junk food when you're busy). Just observe. Let your inner eye be totally wide open and observe *everything* that is going on, both in your outward actions and in your innermost thoughts.

6. When you are ready and feel you have observed all there is to see in your daily life (particularly your daily life with relation to your entrepreneurial project), let yourself begin to gain distance from the scene in front of you. Let your "flying" patterns bring you higher in the sky. Let the minutiae of your daily actions get smaller and smaller, until you are once again at the level of observing the overall idea of your enterprise, and the general way it makes you *feel* day to day.

7. Finally, fly so high that you are no longer even at the level of observing things like business activity, and you have gone to the level of just seeing your life for what it is: an adventure, part of a broader play of consciousness that encompasses the whole of the human community.

8. Open your Workbook to page 62. Without self-censoring, write down what you saw. Do not pass judgment on what you observed, or how you describe the observation. It's okay to write, "I saw myself procrastinating" or "I saw myself being rude with Client X." As always, what you write in the Workbook is for your eyes only, and you're not going to lose any points for observing your own mistakes. In fact, that's the whole point. This is a very important writing exercise, so take as much time as you need to complete it. You may even choose to break down your observations into sections: observations on human interactions, for example, or observations about ways you feel on certain days (or even at certain *times* of day). The magic of the Observer exercise is that we all hold within us the capacity to accurately and completely diagnose our own failings, missteps, and obstacles. Be unabashed in recording your observations, from how you are managing your time to how you are taking out your work frustrations at home. You can even observe yourself as you are recording your observations from the visualization exercise. If you feel, "Oh, no, I keep beating myself up on this stuff, the last thing I need to do is put it in writing," record this as well.

9. Remember also to notice the positive. As you were observing your daily life, you must have seen moments of great joy and evidence of lucidity and success in your professional life. Write these down, too. Focus especially on your courageous moments, when you faced doing something particularly difficult for you. Don't brush over these observations, or make them generalizations (for example, don't let "I took the initiative to speak to my husband about how stressed I was likely to be during our upcoming business launch" become "I was communicative with Bob"). It is critical to be *honest* with yourself. When you are honest with yourself, your creative energy flows without interruption, and breakthroughs can happen. Take as much time as you need to record all your observations, both "good" and "bad."

When you have finished all of your recorded observations, take a break. Go for a run. Watch a movie with your family or friends. Read a few chapters in a novel. Disconnect and take at least a day to come back to this. Put away the kit and do something unrelated for at least twenty-four hours. After that, come back and continue below.

Feelings and Facts

I hope you enjoyed your time away. You should have a little more perspective now. The Observer exercise is more intense than many realize, and on later review, people are often surprised to read what they observed. Now that you have at least a day of distance from your observations, go back to them. Open your Workbook to page 62 and take some time to go over each observation. You may even remember that you observed something you didn't write down, or that what you wrote didn't fully capture a certain observation. It's fine to *add* to your observations, *but don't cross anything out.* Trust that what you wrote then was true to yourself at the time that you wrote it, as much as you now might be tempted to delete what you don't like.

Now, I want you to categorize your observations. Start by breaking them down into two main categories: feelings and facts. The first, sentimental category of observations is more subtle and enigmatic. Feeling observations have to do with your emotional state at a given moment in your daily life rather than what is actually *happening* at the moment of observation. For me, feeling observations include my sense of accomplishment when I finish a project for a client, or my panic and nervousness when I haven't yet reviewed my company's financial accounts at the end of the month. Feeling observations are difficult (and occasionally painful), but they are critical to entrepreneurial growth. The second category of observations you should list in your Workbook—what I call facts—is less about what is going on in the inner world than what is going on in the outer world. Fact observations should be further broken down into problems and solutions. Problems are the dysfunctional patterns and clearly identifiable mistakes you observed in your life: the lack of same-day response to a customer service call, for example, or your failure to get that necessary checkup. Solutions are the behavioral patterns and moments of strength and clarity that solve problems and break down obstacles. For most of this chapter I focus on the facts, but first I'll explore feelings a little bit more.

Feeling Observations

For many of the entrepreneurs whom I have led through the Observer visualization exercise over the years, feeling observations reveal underlying emotional and psychological obstacles in a business project's development that may be obvious in hindsight but that the entrepreneur did not previously acknowledge. As you saw in the last chapter, on entrepreneurial Achilles' heels, emotional and psychological obstacles hold greater sway in our lives than the so-called practical barriers to succeeding in business— lack of start-up financing, for example, or the absence of complementary business partner. The money, worthiness, forgetfulness, holding-on, and expediency traps all have more to do with overcoming psychological barriers than anything else.

Resist the urge to shut out the challenging implications of the feeling observations. Accept the powerful messages they give you. For example, if when performing the Observer exercise, you saw yourself feeling unhappy and unfulfilled in your current job, while your only real moments of exaltation come from going over your new business idea in your head and scheming about the future, well, that's a pretty clear signal it's time to make the leap to do your own thing. Or you might have observed that you are particularly content and joyful when you are interacting with clients, as opposed to managing things back at the office. This could be a sign that you should divvy up responsibilities with a business partner to allow yourself to be "in the field" more. Feeling observations can carry with them transformative messages that tie together the

The Story of Wade

I once worked with an entrepreneur named Wade, who performed the Observer exercise in the midst of a particularly painful financial restructuring of his music-retailing business. When he flew like a bird above his own life and was honest with himself about what he saw, the picture was not so pretty: someone who was stressed most of the time, wasn't sleeping well, wasn't paying attention to his girlfriend, and was trying to hold together the morale of his team while managing his investors' concerns that he was losing money and was in danger of going out of business. While many of these observations also qualify as observations in the fact category, Wade's primary honest reaction to his observations was a simple one of sadness at "not feeling like himself." This qualifies as a feeling observation. What does it mean not to feel "like yourself"? I asked him. "I am *not* naturally an unhappy person," Wade responded, and his eyes brightened as he continued. "I went into this business because I love the adventure of my own business, because I love music, and because I love working with other people who love music." Suddenly, he realized what he had to do: focus on his personal well-being and get closer to what really makes him happy about the music retailing business—the music!

Wade began to really listen to the music again in his life. He proposed to his longtime sweetheart. He downsized the business and brought in other music retailing partners like Best Buy and Virgin Records to help him sell his custom CD consoles, so he could go back to the basics of his music-mixing business—leaving behind the big expansion dreams of certain investors. He began to enjoy himself again as he got back in touch with the aspects of the business that really excited him from the beginning. It's not that he was cavalier about the restructuring steps he needed to take (in fact, his self-possession and contentment made him much more adept at his own financial rescue operation), he just recognized that in order to make progress in his business he first needed to make progress in his life.

practical and the emotional in ways you might not immediately understand.

If the Observer exercise is to be effective at helping you make positive changes in your entrepreneurial path, it's critical to be honest with yourself about your emotional state. A lack of feeling observations in your Workbook is a bad sign, probably the result of suppressing your emotions. If you've got that nagging sensation in the back of your head that you haven't fully explored your feeling observations, you may want to try the Observer exercise again before moving on to further explore your fact observations.

Fact Observations: Problems

It's the simple stuff that gets us, and everyone who's been honest with himself or herself seems to observe problem-creating behaviors in the Observer exercise that often have very simple causes: a shoddy client presentation from staying up too late the night before, or slow customer growth due to procrastination in developing decent marketing materials. Problem observations are not as insidious or deeply rooted as the entrepreneurial Achilles' heels you studied in the last chapter, although they are symptomatic of these deeper weaknesses: Burnout from taking on too many things at once is a typical problem observation, whereas the holding-on trap is the underlying cause of the problem.

In general, the good thing about problem observations is that they are eminently fixable. If we can clearly identify our dysfunctional behavior, we can usually apply the appropriate remedy. (Even if the remedy is not immediately apparent, just seeing and recognizing the problem can be liberating.) This is why the Observer exercise is so important: It is the most efficient way to bring to the surface our correctable mistakes and behavioral dysfunctions, so we can apply practical solutions to our problems.

Fact Observations: Solutions

Some of your prospective solutions may come from the Observer exercise itself. To paraphrase the great entrepreneur's philosopher Kierkegaard, within every human frailty lie the seeds of its cure. As Kierkegaard understood (and denoted by the title of Chapter 2, "Your Strength May Be Your Weakness"), the paradox of humanity is that many of these solutions are in fact the flip side of certain problem observations. Take, for example, the retail entrepreneur who observes himself experiencing mood swings at the store and voicing personal frustrations to employees and customers (a problem observation). Given his willingness to show emotion on the job, his business is also likely to be a close-knit team, where personal bonds are encouraged (a solution observation). Or the graphic designer who observes herself getting lost in and completely confused by the need to manage accounting programs for the first time as a sole proprietor (problem). She is also likely to be the one who finds herself reaching out to find a complementary business partner who is comfortable with numbers and allows her to focus on her artistic strengths (solution).

Being Honest with Yourself

Recently I had the opportunity to consult with Diego, an aspiring entrepreneur. At our first meeting, Diego complained about his dilemma: He could not decide whether to continue on his safe path working in a decently paid (and well-regarded) government post or to make the leap full-time into a start-up project he had been thinking about for some time. Like many people in this situation, Diego was spending almost as much time agonizing over the decision as actually researching his entrepreneurial project.

I strongly believe that most of the time the "big" decisions in our lives are really foils that we hide behind—the decision is already made, deep within, and we must summon the courage to dig and find it. So I led

Diego through the Observer exercise. We started with the feeling observations: What did he feel like when sitting at his desk at work? Working on his project after hours? What fears was he having about leaving his regular job? Were they monetary? Reputational? Perhaps related to the prospect of actually discovering whether he was "good enough" to be on his own? I encouraged Diego to let himself observe his feelings in his professional life without any bias. He was not to report on the feelings he liked, was proud of, or thought he *should* have, but to report on what he actually observed. Then I had him focus on fact observations—both the problem and solution areas of his daily experience. I asked him to pay particular attention to those solution observations that seemed to defuse his feelings of fear.

The results were remarkable. Diego and I both expected that he would observe himself most "at peace" or "inspired" when working on his start-up project, and that the Observer exercise would help him develop the clarity of purpose to make the leap. In fact, the outcome was nearly opposite! Diego saw himself inspired by the basic parameters of his government job, which involves complex macroeconomic research and financial modeling. He also recognized his and his family's pride in his professional accomplishments. The most salient solution observation was that he observed himself most "at peace" when working on the business plan for his entrepreneurial project *while* secure in his current job. He also found that he had been suppressing serious doubts about the viability of his start-up idea.

Conclusion: It made no sense for Diego to leave his job at that time. His entrepreneurial endeavor was functioning as a creative outlet for him— a signal, perhaps, that he should seek entrepreneurial opportunities with the agency where he worked, or maybe it was a project he was destined to embark on in the future.

As it turned out, the latter would be true. By freeing up his mental energy from the constant debate over whether to leave his day job, Diego was able to really indulge his creative impulse and tinker significantly with his start-up plan. He began to ask for others' input, unafraid now of getting into a discussion about whether he intended to leave his job—he didn't. Lo and behold, this new level of openness led to significant changes in his entrepreneurial project, a much higher level of confidence in its viability, and, ultimately, a decision to make the leap—much more happily and confidently than he would have before.

Whatever your entrepreneurial path, rest assured that at some point your strengths will manifest weaknesses, and your weaknesses will become the areas from which many exciting changes will emerge. The Observer exercise allows you to observe what is working well in your business life and pinpoint your strengths. By clearly identifying solutions, or fruitful patterns in your life (you're more effective in meetings on Mondays and Tuesdays than Thursdays and Fridays; you're at your sharpest when you interact face-to-face rather than on the phone), you put yourself in the position to build and focus on these strengths. Put simply: To help you get better at what you do (and even enjoy it more), start by observing what already works for you—what you do "right."

I have been leading entrepreneurs and business executives through the Observer visualization exercise for a number of years. Although feeling observations tend to be the most powerful in their potential for personal transformation, I find that most people feel more comfortable in the realm of problems and solutions—however idiosyncratic these may be. (I once had a participant in a seminar who claimed to observe himself at his most effective working from bed at eleven in the morning, and another whose primary problem observation was an inability to get *angry* at his clients!) The key is to find which approach works best for *you,* hence the importance of categorizing your observations into feelings and facts. It's akin to the difference between right-brain/left-brain thinking. As you go through the Observer exercise next time (like the other exercises in this kit, it is meant to be used again and again), focus on either a practical or emotional stance, whichever feels more productive to you. Either stance will get you to the same ultimate goal. When you've done the Observer exercise with enough people, you begin to see certain patterns emerge over and over. The important thing to realize about the Observer exercise—whether through feeling or fact—is that by removing our normal defenses, it allows us to see our lives plainly and provides the necessary *context* for very practical advice to sink in.

The Ten Most Common Areas of Observation

After doing the Observer exercise with hundreds of entrepreneurs, I have begun to recognize certain patterns that appear over and over. Following are the ten most common—and important—areas of observation for entrepreneurs. I have distilled the practical insights I have gleaned from years of listening to the real-life observations of hundreds of entrepreneurs in this list, and in the Observation Cards for this chapter I provide more detailed guidance for each subject. These areas of observation are listed in rough order of emergence—that is, when in the entrepreneurial life cycle they tend to become salient. If while reading these topics, you detect that the main areas of entrepreneurial observation fall into the "mundane, boring" category, as opposed to the "inspirational, motivational" category, you are right indeed! That's the point of this chapter: tethering our camels.

1. Partnering with Family and Friends

At almost every seminar I have given on entrepreneurship—from sessions on "Learning from Failure" to lectures on "Approaches to Early Stage Capitalization"—the same question comes up: "Do you think it's a good idea to start a business with family and friends?" Given the fact that more than two-thirds of all businesses in the United States are started by close friends or family members working in partnership, it is a bit like asking, "Do you think it is a good idea to get married?" In either case, people's experiences—and the high rates of both marriage and business failure—

clearly indicate that the answer is, "It depends." People often ask for my personal observations on this subject, given that the relationship I had with my friend and cofounder of our govWorks business was the primary subject of a feature-length documentary. I even hired my father in one of the businesses I started. In a sense, I have voted with my feet on this issue (in favor, that is, of going into business with family members and friends); after the govWorks experience I started a second business with my former partner and longtime friend, Tom Herman, and he is still my business partner to this day. At the same time, I have seen many other such situations fail, at times nearly from the outset.

It is clear that the business partnerships of any kind that work most effectively are those that are governed by clear, mutually agreed on ground rules. One of my clients, a father-son team managing a heavy-equipment-leasing company, is able to make the relationship work because both the father and the son have clearly divided up the responsibilities in the business (the former focusing on client relationship management and sales, and the latter focusing on internal operations and finance). Even more important, each has agreed on where they will be with respect to the business five and ten years down the road (the father will be semiretired, and the son will be CEO but will have hired a senior sales chief to accompany him in his leadership of the business). My strong advice in the case of business partnerships with friends and loved ones is lay out the ground rules up front and make sure all parties have signed on to them. Unlike marriage, where prenuptial agreements are controversial and sometimes counterproductive, in business, prenuptials are highly advised; in fact, I would even say they're a must. The general rule to apply on the topics to cover in such an agreement is what I call the "discomfort rule": Anything where just thinking about discussing it with your family member/friend/business partner makes you uncomfortable is exactly what needs to be discussed and agreed on ahead of time. Commonly, this includes who decides what the capital structure looks like, who decides what products to sell and to which kind of customers you're selling them, and who decides whom to hire and fire. By resounding majority, business partnerships with friends and loved ones that work smoothly and successfully are those where the tough issues of power-sharing and decision-making authority are fleshed out ahead of time, *before* they come to a head in the context of daily operations. See Observation Cards 1 and 2 for more tips on how to successfully approach such arrangements with family and friends, and refer to your Workbook to note related observations.

2. Organizing Your Time

Time, as the saying goes, is the most precious commodity. This maxim is truer for the entrepreneur than any salaried professional. The entrepreneur is constantly being pulled in many directions, by the needs of clients, vendors, partners, employees, lenders, and investors, not to mention family members and his or her own personal interests. Unlike in a traditional working environment, most entrepreneurs don't have a boss who dictates their use of time and in what order of priority they should be attending to their various stakeholders. The entrepreneur is therefore confronted with the daily challenge of choosing whose needs to attend to first and whose to put off for another day. This challenge is compounded by the common entrepreneurial trait of trying to please everybody all

> *"Until you value yourself, you will not value your time. Until you value your time, you will not do anything with it."*
> —M. Scott Peck

the time, otherwise known as the inability to say no. It is remarkable how many entrepreneurs' success and failure in their businesses comes down to the seemingly simple issue of how they organize their time. Successful entrepreneurs know how to say no and carve out time for seemingly nonpriority activities like strategic planning, product development, and, yes, even time out with their family.

I have yet to meet a successful entrepreneur—from personalities as different as Strauss Zelnick (Zelnick Media), Marc Andreesen (Netscape), or Alan Patricof (APAX)—who does not in large part attribute his or her success to an ability to jealously guard and structure his or her time. Jeff Bezos, the colorful founder of Amazon.com, for example, takes meetings only on Mondays, Wednesdays, and Fridays, and devotes Tuesdays and Thursdays to catching up on correspondence and "just thinking." Winston Churchill, the consummate entrepreneur in a politician's body (who quite creatively worked himself up from a journalist's assistant in the Boer War to the British prime ministership), used to devote certain hours of each day to discrete activities. In the midst of the chaos of war, he would still discuss social policy between 2 and 3 in the afternoon and war machinations between 4 and 7 o'clock. He would also take a late-afternoon nap every day followed by a bath. Lunch and dinner would always be accompanied by champagne.

Entrepreneurs are free-spirited by nature, notoriously difficult to pin down, and resistant to all attempts (even self-imposed ones) to introduce structure and discipline to their daily schedule. All the more important, then, that you make a concerted effort to modify the scattershot tendency of your daily routine. Your success at organizing and *prioritizing* your own time will be perhaps the greatest predictor of your overall success as an entrepreneur. See

Observation Cards 3 and 4 for some dos and don'ts of this essential exercise, and refer to your Workbook to note any related observations.

3. Paperwork and Ground Rules

In the previous section on partnering with friends and family, I alluded to the importance of setting "rules of engagement" at the outset. The same is true, really, of going into business with *anyone.* Most entrepreneurs are notoriously bad at what they consider the minutiae of business: incorporation documents, partnership agreements, employment agreements, and other such fun stuff. Although you'll rarely get an entrepreneur to admit it, my experience has shown that half of all entrepreneurs feel that such detailed legal agreements and contracts are *beneath* them—one of those things that obsessive lawyers and accountants (no offense to lawyers and accountants, many of whom are entrepreneurs themselves) are there for. The other 50 percent of entrepreneurs see the detailed work of business documentation to be *above* them—over their heads. This latter group of entrepreneurs is composed mainly of those who know the importance of documentation and paperwork but who find the whole prospect of contract negotiation and legalese overwhelming. The problem here is more serious than it might appear: I am talking not only about entrepreneurs' proclivity to gloss over necessary corporate documentation (I have seen more entrepreneurs than I can count who have been in business for years and still have never properly incorporated or done any real tax planning!); I am also talking about a tendency to avoid even basic *conversations* with stakeholders that address critical issues like potential breach of respective responsibilities, financial redress for breach (in other words, who would owe what to whom if someone didn't do what he or she was supposed to do), and contractual termination (in other words, what happens when we decide not to work together anymore).

Entrepreneurs are by nature optimists, and the same resistance to prenuptials mentioned in the above section on partnering with family and friends also makes itself felt in the area of documentation and rules setting in general. You must take remedial steps if you have shoddy documentation, or poor communication on sensitive subjects, like breach of contract. This is a classic example of not tethering your camel, and an untethered camel in this department can often lead to a new business's downfall. Too many entrepreneurs lose their core clientele or run out of cash because they neglect to file a patent to protect their invention, or don't anticipate how much it would cost to defend themselves in a frivolous lawsuit from a disgruntled former partner. These are the realities of business that you must plan for, although, like most entrepreneurs, you are probably not wired to think about the downside of your entrepreneurial adventure. Even if it takes hiring a lawyer or another professional to be the pessimist to your optimist, you need to take the necessary steps to get your documentation right and put ground rules in order. See Observation Cards 5–15 for a more detailed road map to the different types of protective documentation and contracts you need to think about as a small-business owner, and refer to your Workbook to note any related observations.

4. Outside Professional Service Providers

Documentation and paperwork leads naturally into the seemingly mundane territory of lawyers, accountants, bankers, public relations people, and the other outside service providers the typical entrepreneur uses over his or her business lifetime. Although this may not at first seem to qualify as one of the most important areas of observation, my years of working with entrepreneurs belie this notion. In fact, the comfort and effectiveness with which an entrepreneur makes use of outside service providers is the subject of some of the most acutely positive *and* negative observations that I hear about in my seminars. My grandfather, an old entrepreneur himself, used to say there are only four relationships that you must seek out to be happy in your life: your spouse, your best friend, your lawyer, and your accountant. (Unfortunately, he didn't always list them in that order.) There is a lot of truth in this advice from a man who came to Ellis Island in 1947 with the proverbial $10 in his pocket and only a speck of English. Your lawyer and your accountant are there to help you translate your entrepreneurial dream into the language of business. Show me a serious entrepreneur who hasn't spent significant time with a lawyer and an accountant, and I will give you an entrepreneur who has never experienced any real growth in his or her business and is not equipped for future success. As contrary as it is to the grand scheming and passion-infused motivations of the prototypical entrepreneur, the banality of strong and trusted relationships with outside experts is essential.

As your business grows, you may get to the point where you have your own internal general counsel (lawyer) or controller (accountant), but even then you need to have outside advice and perspective.

At different points in your business's developmental path, you are likely to need other outside help as well; from public relations professionals to investment bankers and others. The key is to make these relationships a priority and understand that your ultimate success will depend on focusing on what you're best at doing (what a Harvard Business School professor would call your "core competencies"), while delegating or outsourcing everything else. For tips on everything from interviewing your first lawyer to deciding when/if you need a public relations firm on retainer, refer to Observation Cards 16–17 and refer to your Workbook to note any related observations.

5. Goal Setting: Operational and Personal

Most legends, from Homer's *Odyssey* to J. R. R. Tolkien's *Lord of the Rings*, are about the pursuit of a nearly unattainable goal. The hero always seems to possess both naïveté about the probably negative outcome of the quest and a dogged determination to journey on until the end, even if it means death along the way. The entrepreneur's life is arguably not so dissimilar from the legendary hero's in the difficulty of the task and in the determination to achieve it.

> "The world makes way for the man who knows where he is going."
> —Ralph Waldo Emerson

Yet I am constantly amazed at what I have come to call the entrepreneurial disconnect: Although nearly all entrepreneurs say they are "determined to make it," "willing to scale the highest mountain," or some other hyperbolic phrase to describe the quest for their particular Holy Grail, remarkably few have taken the trouble to identify *what* exactly it is they are looking for! I have not yet figured out why this is the case, but entrepreneurs are chronically bad at articulating and setting goals— whether grand goals like, "What do I want out of life?" or more mundane milestones like, "What revenue numbers are we trying to hit next month?" Can you imagine Jason saying, "Hmm, what was it that I was after again? Something about a fleece, wasn't it?"

Many of the most successful entrepreneurs are, of course, fanatical about goal-setting (Michael Dell is said to get revenue and product shipment goals by the day. Andrew Carnegie would write his business plans twenty years in advance!), but this is most often a learned trait. I think there is something about setting operational milestones (how many people you're going to hire next year, how many new clients you're going to have, or how many stores you're going to open) that makes entrepreneurs feel a little queasy, as if the exercise of goal setting itself might convert the ethereal magic of the entrepreneur's dream into something concrete and banal—like the irrational fear that small children have of telling you their birthday wish.

In any event, to be successful, you *must* be disciplined about setting and achieving goals for your development, and not just in the traditional sense of revenue and profit milestones, or product shipments and store openings. You must also set goals for yourself in terms of where'd you like to be *personally* in relation to your business project one year, three years, or even ten years out. When are you finally going to quit your day job and make the leap to start your own thing? Do you want to be running the business over the long term, or do you want to bring in operating partners? Over time, do you want to focus more on client acquisition or more on product development? These are goal-setting exercises as well. Keep your primary currency in mind when setting overarching goals (i.e., if you're healthdriven, "50 percent annual gross sales growth over the next ten years" might not be the best goal). For more guidance on what milestones to focus on, and how to implement goal setting into your entrepreneurial life, see Observation Cards 18 and 19. Refer to your Workbook to note any related observations.

6. Financial Budgeting and Planning

Entrepreneurs tend to have plenty of inspiration and motivation (if you think you lack in these areas, it's unlikely you would have picked up this kit in the first place—so you can relax). The main challenge for entrepreneurs is to support their high-flying dreams and aspirations with a solid foundation of time management, legal documentation, goal setting, planning, and budgeting. Let's now discuss the last two of these. In the Observer exercise you performed earlier in the chapter, you were asked to fly pretty low, so to speak, and observe your daily entrepreneurial endeavors in as much detail as possible. Based on previous observer visualizations with hundreds of entrepreneurs in varying stages of business development, I know it is pretty likely that you made some observation (whether of the feeling or fact variety) concerning financial planning and budgeting. For many entrepreneurs, this is the most challenging part of managing their own business. Because the financial data of fledgling businesses are by nature private (and their precariousness might actually cause fright in loved ones and close business associates), most entrepreneurs have difficulty reaching out for help in this area.

You must be careful of this tendency to keep things too close to the vest and therefore shut yourself off from valuable feedback and guidance. Earlier, I covered the need for a trusted outside accountant, even in a start-up business. Although your accountant is indeed critical for tax planning and the preparation of financial statements, you also need either to learn how to develop financial spreadsheets yourself for planning purposes, or find a trusted associate or business partner who can do this for you. Even at the earliest stage, businesses should be following a written financial plan of some sort. Flying by the seat of your pants, or doing post-factum accounting (that is, looking mostly at how you did last month, as opposed to how you're going to do next month and the month after) is not acceptable; it is a recipe for failure. For tips on basic financial modeling, as well as a list of resources for outside help from firms and professional associations, see Observation Cards 20 and 21. Refer to your Workbook to note any related observations.

7. Raising Money

In the mid-1990s, a fundamental shift took place in the small-business financing environment in the United States. Before then, about 90 percent of start-up business capital came from commercial lenders, mostly neighborhood banks and factoring agencies. Most of the other 10 percent came from friends and family, effectively people chipping in a little here and there to help someone get a business off the ground, and a tiny percentage (1–2 percent at most) came from "professional" investors: venture capital firms. Starting in the 1990s, there was an explosion in so-called venture capital. Institutional venture capital, while a thriving industry in certain communities since the late '60s and early '70s (like Silicon Valley, south of San Francisco, and the Route 128 semicircle around the Boston metro area), was effectively nonexistent prior to the boom in early stage technology, telecommunications, and biotech investing in the late '90s.

Venture capital is like "friends and family" money except that it comes from a professional company whose only purpose is to invest capital in high-risk start-up businesses. This money almost always comes in the form of "equity capital" (which means it entitles the investing venture capital fund to a part ownership in the start-up business, as opposed to just a debt that it is owed, such as a bank loan), and usually venture capital firms take an active role in a new business's development. While entrepreneurs have had to "dance for dollars," as a friend of mine puts it, since time immemorial, the options available to the entrepreneur—or the number of folks willing to pay for the dance, so to speak—have expanded dramatically over the last decade or so.

This is not necessarily a good thing, however. As discussed in the last chapter, the tendency to make all new developments in your business dependent on whether you can raise money can be deadly, and there is certainly something to be said for bootstrapping a start-up business. However, the benefits of outside debt and equity venture capital can include more rapid time-to-market with new products, the ability to grow more quickly, and the capacity to better manage working capital hiccups that kill many start-up businesses. As a result, many entrepreneurs spend half of their time or more on the road, dancing for dollars from friends and family, banks, and venture capital firms. For a step-by-step guide on how to effectively approach the money-raising trail without losing focus on your business, and how to successfully integrate lenders and investors into your business's capital structure, see Observation Cards 22–34. Refer to your Workbook to note any related observations.

8. Focus, Focus, Focus

Years ago, I had a conversation with David Rockefeller that changed my approach to business. David, who sponsored a scholarship at Harvard that helped me get through that (very expensive) school and founded an organization called the New York City Partnership, was the first significant outside financial backer of my second business. His book, *Memoirs*, is also one of the best business-oriented autobiographies you will find, and for all of these reasons I see him as a mentoring force in my life. So it was with some nervousness that I approached him at a formal dinner a few years back to solicit some nugget of wisdom. Stumbling a bit over my prepared question, I ended up simply asking him for his secret to success. "Focus," he responded. I sought more context. "Can you tell me more?" I asked. "Focus," he said again. I once again asked for more information: "And–" I began. "Focus," he interrupted me for the last time.

If there is one lesson that every entrepreneur should hear each and every single day upon awakening, it's David Rockefeller's "focus, focus, focus." It goes back to my comments on time management. Entrepreneurs simply try to do too much. We bite off more than we can chew. We try to please too many people at once. We try to release too many products at once. We take on too many clients at once. We try to fit in too many things on the schedule at once. We even try to read too many entrepreneurial guidebooks at once. In a large sense, it matters more that we pick *one* thing to focus on in our business at a given time than what exactly that one thing is. We need to learn how to focus on one thing at a time, and focus entirely on it until we achieve it, and then we can move on. Entrepreneurial success is much less about the brilliance of a given new business idea than it is about the laserlike focus that leads to successful execution of that idea. Starbucks was the sixth or seventh funky coffeehouse that sprung up in Seattle around the same time, over twenty years ago. Howard Schultz, however, understood David Rockefeller's mantra, and the results speak for themselves. Although Starbucks now carries CDs and lemonade, he focused first and foremost on selling gourmet coffee. For more help on focusing and prioritization techniques for your business, see Observation Cards 35 and 36, and refer to your Workbook to note any related observations.

9. Mergers, Acquisitions, Strategic Partnerships, and Other Scary Steps

There are certain things in life that people tend to keep secret. Plastic surgery comes to mind. So does the use of Rogaine or Viagra. Although you would think that business issues wouldn't be considered quite so personal or potentially embarrassing, mergers and acquisitions activity is one of those things that people are chronically afraid to talk about or seek outside counsel on. For some reason, entrepreneurs tend to follow a pattern of closing themselves down to outside advice more and more as their businesses get larger and larger. This is a bit like an open heart surgeon getting increasingly resistant to learning from other doctors as he or she performed more and more complicated operations.

This doesn't make sense, of course. But it's what entrepreneurs do all the time. When they first embark on the entrepreneurial journey—setting up shop and incorporating for the first time, or pitching for the first client—they are open to help from other entrepreneurs, even from us entrepreneurial guidebook writers. But as their businesses grow, they close down to outside advice, and a bunker mentality sets in. After working with dozens of entrepreneurs suffering from bunker mentality, I have concluded that it is the result of two unrelated phenomena: first, the natural egotism that often accompanies a certain degree of outward success; second, entrepreneurs' growing fear that any success occurred *in spite* of their own knowledge base, and that if they turn to others for guidance they will betray their ignorance, especially as the stakes get higher.

The need for help on mergers and acquisitions is one of those things that do not typically happen in the early stages of an enterprise's development. But as a young business achieves some momentum and size, it will sometimes receive an offer to be purchased by a larger entity, or a big company will come knocking on its door to explore possibilities for a strategic partnership or cross-selling arrangement of some kind. These are precious moments in a business's (and an entrepreneur's) evolution. These are the moments when a small business can break through to the next level of development and grow to become a midsize business and—someday—a truly big business. Knowing how to handle these unsolicited offers, or knowing when in your development to approach other companies to purchase (or be purchased), is a critical ingredient to large-scale success in the marketplace. There are hundreds of competent and reasonably priced strategic advisory firms out there (my own firm, Recognition Group, being an example) that offer just this sort of help. The hardest part is reaching out. For guidance on when and to whom to reach out for help on big strategic steps in your business's evolution, refer to Observation Cards 37–40. Refer to your Workbook to note any related observations.

10. Handing Off the Baton: Outside Management and Boards

Now that we have entered the delicate territory of entrepreneurial egotism and reaching out for help, it is best to address one of the most intractable problem areas: delegation. Entrepreneurs are almost genetically incapable of properly delegating. I have touched on this several times already, from the ways trying to do too much negatively affects time management to the use of outside professional service providers for effective financial planning and budgeting. But the consummate act of delegation also may be the most important in a business's development: handing the leadership baton to someone other than yourself. While nearly every book written on entrepreneurship emphasizes that the most successful entrepreneurs know when to hand off the CEO or COO post for the sake of the enterprise's long-term development, nine out of ten entrepreneurs still show a stubborn resistance and an ingrained opposition to this supreme act of delegation or transfer of authority. And it's not only in the grandest sense of handing off the baton of leadership; this resistance and fear are prevalent as well when it comes to recruiting outside board members and official advisers for a growing business. Although many entrepreneurs give lip service to the idea of a diversified board of directors that can give them guidance and advice, most balk at actually involving outsiders in their business in any meaningful way. Yet it is one of the most salutary things you can do for your business.

Outside directors and advisers, even outside (or, as they're sometimes called, "professional") chief executive, chief operating officer, and chief financial officer, almost always provide rocket fuel for a young business's development. They provide you with wise counsel, and (if you give them some sort of equity stake in your growing business, which is advisable) their presence immediately expands the number of highly competent professionals who are directly motivated to see you succeed. The most successful and enlightened entrepreneurs see board building and handing off the baton of operating executive leadership even while remaining involved in other areas as moments to be embraced and celebrated along the evolutionary road to large-scale success. Of course, it is important to recognize that some entrepreneurs never want to grow big. If you want to remain a sole proprietorship or a very small business, soliciting some sort of outside board member or official adviser is *still* highly recommended. For more guidance on how to build your board of directors or advisers, and/or identify when the time has come to bring outside senior executive officers into your company, see Observation Cards 41–44. Refer to your Workbook to note any related observations.

Chapter 3 Conclusion

You are close to successfully completing another chapter in your five-part lesson plan. Before moving on to the next chapter—in which I explore further the entrepreneur's challenge to focus, focus, focus—make sure to spend time going over all Observation Cards, and do the Workbook exercises corresponding to each area of observation. Zero in on whichever areas are most relevant to you, based on your observer visualization and the current circumstances of your entrepreneurial project. Even if a particular area of observation doesn't apply to your current stage of entrepreneurial development, spend some time on the subject and study the Observation Card. This will help you prepare for tomorrow's practical challenge. The audio tracks on the *Exercises and Visualizations* CDs corresponding to Chapter 3, "Believe in God but Tether Your Camel," will support the practical elements of this chapter with a couple of variations on the Observer visualization exercise. I encourage you to use the Observer visualization exercise throughout the different stages of your entrepreneurial development. Each time, by flying like a bird over your entrepreneurial daily life, you will gain needed perspective on your current challenges and their prospective solutions.

Chapter 4: Beware the Butterfly Swarm

Staying Focused and Implementing Your Business Plan

Recap

You are making great progress on your journey of entrepreneurial self-examination. As I said at the outset, the process is not easy, and—if you've been keeping your mind and heart open to critique—it's likely to involve certain painful realizations. In the first chapter, I explored the forces that motivate our entrepreneurial strivings—the currencies that impel us to go to work in the morning, overcome obstacles in our path, and forge our dreams into reality.

Currencies

1. Money
2. Recognition
3. Courage
4. Victory
5. Acceptance
6. Health

By being totally honest with ourselves about our primary currency, and identifying where other forces (or secondary currencies) are at work in our lives, we can learn to wield their full power and avoid their attendant liabilities. This is the first step in successful entrepreneurship: self-knowledge.

In the second chapter, I explored the dangers and pitfalls on the battlefield of entrepreneurship—our Achilles' heels of vulnerability and self-sabotage—and explored ways of overcoming them.

You should think of the currencies, Achilles' heels, and areas of

Traps/Achilles' Heels

1. Money trap
2. Worthiness trap
3. Forgetfulness trap
4. Holding-on trap
5. Expediency trap

We fall into these traps when we lose our moorings—in particular, when we are out of tune or in denial with respect to our underlying currencies. Again, it is self-knowledge—the awareness of these Achilles' heels—that keeps us from being hurt by each currency's double-edged sword.

Armed with an appreciation for our principal currencies, and a wariness of the patterns of self-sabotage to which we are all vulnerable, the third chapter began our journey into the quotidian realities of our specific entrepreneurial project. Here, you opened yourself up to disassociated observation of your daily professional life and began to zero in on the most important arenas of activity—or of battle, if you will.

Areas of Observation

1. Partnering with family and friends
2. Organizing your time
3. Paperwork and ground rules
4. Outside professional service providers
5. Goal setting: Operational and personal
6. Financial budgeting and planning
7. Raising money
8. Focus, focus, focus
9. Mergers, acquisitions, strategic partnerships, and other scary steps
10. Handing off the baton: outside management and boards

These ten areas of observation cover a vast swath of the landscape of any entrepreneurial project, and you looked at successful strategies for dealing with each one of them.

observation of Chapters 1–3 as tools you can use in the entrepreneurial fray. They are always at your disposal, and you can draw on them again and again. When you are feeling demotivated, lock into the raw "juice," or power, of your primary currency. If you are feeling out of whack or obsessed with a particular challenge in the entrepreneurial path, it might be that you need actively to seek to balance your primary currency with a complementary, secondary driver—money with health, for example. If you are feeling confused or stuck in your business's development, try to look at the situation objectively and see if you might be falling victim to the forgetfulness trap or the holding-on trap. The lessons of the areas of observation, if you are attuned to them, will come up nearly every day in the course of your start-up or fledgling business. Keep the Observation Cards handy so you can refer to them as you confront the challenges of your day. As a famous nineteenth-century educator once said, "Learning is the domain of repetition and remembrance." Disciplined and constant remembrance of your entrepreneurial toolbox—currencies, Achilles' heels, and areas of observation—is key.

In Chapter 4, we go from learning to *doing*. Having gone through the necessary first steps of self-exploration (currencies, Achilles' heels) and behavioral pattern recognition (areas of observation), you are now ready to study the right way to focus in on a business idea, put together a business plan, and implement a business plan. The first step, as David Rockefeller said, is focus, focus, focus.

Step 1. Inspiration and Focus

The Butterfly Swarm

Growing up, my mother and I lived in the country and regularly took long walks in the woods and the fields around our house. She was content to bask in nature's glory, but I was a boy, and I wanted to chase things. The butterflies were my favorite. I remember one small blue species that would appear seemingly overnight to carpet the path, their little tongues darting into the damp dirt for minerals. The next week, the monarchs would arrive. I'd run through the field to raise them in an orange-and-black swarm. Then I'd stop and watch one individual butterfly, training my eye on it, struggling to keep it in sight and not mix it up with any of the others. Later in the season, when there were fewer butterflies around, I would follow a single butterfly for as long as I could, as it alighted on flowers and bushes and was lifted and dropped by currents of warm air. I'd try to learn the pattern, size, and—I imagined—the personality of that one particular insect. I could never do it for more than a few minutes. My chosen butterfly would melt into the swarm, or begin to look dull and gray compared to its neighbor, and I'd switch allegiance. Tracing my movements from above would have rendered something random and incomprehensible, like scribbles on an Etch-A-Sketch. I can't think of a better metaphor for what commonly afflicts the entrepreneur at the font of inspiration.

In the beginning, inspiration is like that swarm of butterflies. Your eye and your heart follow it, swept up in its beauty. Then the dispersion begins. The color and movement become individual butterflies, as inspiration becomes idea. The idea becomes increasingly specific, breaking into components. The entrepreneur must pick a butterfly squadron, or even one particular butterfly, so as to not get lost in the chaos. But entrepreneurs are not good at this kind of focus. We are easily enthralled and get lost as a more beautiful butterfly whizzes by, distracting us for a split second from the one we had been tracking and is now suddenly gone. We tend to focus, yes, but on the most beautiful idea of the moment, and we flit from one to the other, trying to re-create the rush of our original epiphany. The issue is not determination, or even focused energy. The problem lies in the tendency to get carried away and to want to track the whole swarm, to be the one to view every wing and every pattern more closely and more successfully than the next guy.

You must learn to control your impulse to get caught up in the butterfly swarm. You must pick an idea—often a more limited version of your original concept—and stick with it. Specificity is your friend. Keep narrowing down your original concept until you hit the bedrock of a concrete first-step plan. If you are considering a dry-cleaning business, focus in on one neighborhood, or even on a specialty such as wedding gowns. If you are launching an executive-coaching business, focus in on executives in the pharmaceutical industry. If you already run a small-appliance and electronics dealership, focus in on high-end installation jobs. As an entrepreneur, you are wired to think big. You need to limit this impulse, at least in the beginning, in order to successfully engage in profitable commerce from near the get-go. From this successful starting point, you will be able to build. Don't worry that you are not conquering the world on day one. Focus your original idea enough so you simply live as a business to see day *two* and day *three*. Eventually, you will conquer the world. But you need to start somewhere.

Nearly every time I review an entrepreneur's business plan, I am struck by the need to further focus the idea. Often, I ask an aspiring entrepreneur to come back two, three, even four times with revised versions of the original idea until I feel it is focused enough to use to create a more specific operating launch plan. The toughest part of the focusing exercise is giving up some of the grandiosity of the original plan. You may start with the idea of creating a *different* kind of high-end travel agency—one that creates opportunities for community service, or total cultural immersion in the host country—but by the time you have opened your small storefront on Peachtree Street with an initial expertise in Ecuadorian ecotrips and a tiny clientele, it may not feel so grand anymore. In the next section of this chapter, I discuss the importance of planning through these painful early stages, and of sticking with it (a never-say-die attitude and the ability to endure are part and parcel of every successful entrepreneur's personality). But for the moment, consider the example of Berenice.

The Story of Berenice

Berenice is the daughter of Holocaust survivors who fled Europe and landed on the coast of Brazil in the late 1940s. Berenice's parents showed up with essentially nothing in their pockets and no knowledge of Portuguese. Berenice was born there and raised in a household where her father worked himself to the bone trying to re-create the successful accounting business they had back in Poland before the war. Despite the language barrier, and the natural obstacles that exist to any newcomer in a foreign land, Berenice's father was able to build a small accounting practice in Rio de Janeiro. It produced enough income to keep Berenice and her siblings off the streets (and working in the family business, of course) and put Berenice through college.

All her life, Berenice saw her father—an incredibly bright and respected man back in his own country—eke out a living in devotion to his family. Berenice cultivated an inner desire to "graduate" from her father's school of entrepreneurship, using her native understanding of the business culture and her hard-earned degrees in engineering and mathematics to launch a business that could be many times the size of her father's and provide the whole family (not only her parents but also her future children and grandchildren) with financial security and peace of mind. Immediately after finishing her graduate studies, Berenice dove into the entrepreneurial fray, raising a nice sum of money and hiring more than thirty people within a short period of time. Berenice's accounting practice, she told herself, would be more professionally managed than her father's and service the midmarket and large Brazilian conglomerates that her father only aspired to approach.

But Berenice's dreams quickly came crashing down. She hadn't focused her accountancy on any particular industry, geography, or even developmental stage of her target clients and was trying to be everything to everyone. The result was a lack of necessary expertise on given assignments within the staff and a lack of direction in marketing and client acquisition. When Berenice went out of business in the late 1980s, it was her father who bailed her out of a couple of dangling obligations: an office lease and some unpaid taxes. The little, conservative, chug-along business ended up coming to the rescue of the grandly planned start-up.

Looking at Berenice's experience, you might be tempted to glean the moral of the story as don't set your sights too high, or don't get too big for your britches. But Berenice's problem was *not* that her dreams were too grand. Her motivation to carry the vision of her father to the next level, and support her family, was raw and powerful. It is just this kind of deep-seated motivation (in Berenice's case, the currency of courage stemming from her desire to be the hero of her family) that provides the fuel for entrepreneurial success. Berenice's problem was that she never refined her inspirational idea. She never focused it in on a specific business plan that could be measured against concrete milestones and executed in identifiable steps.

The next time around the entrepreneurial track, Berenice learned from her mistakes and took a different path. In the early 1990s, she started another business. This time, she spent almost two years developing her business plan after hours, while working as a part-time systems consultant for a Brazilian energy company. She realized that her previous infatuation with starting an accounting business was driven more by her father's shadow than by her own personal interests. She also realized that she needed to suppress her desire to be the "savior" of her family overnight and accept her current station in life, as a struggling thirty-year-old aspiring entrepreneur, to focus on laying the groundwork for long-term success.

Without articulating it to herself, Berenice was going through an exercise of discovering her own primary currency and cultivating complementary tendencies. The result of her extended introspection was the emergence of a plan to develop a consulting business oriented toward helping large Brazilian companies realize cost savings in their supply chain. Berenice realized that she liked working on computer systems and databases more than she liked accounting, and that what she was really good at was finding mistakes—accounting entry errors, delivery batch mismatches—in gobs of information. She knew she could be successful starting a business that capitalized on this innate skill. But having learned what can happen when you spring too quickly out of the starting gate, she didn't hire a bunch of people, attack the whole marketplace, or open an office straightaway.

Berenice decided initially to focus her new "efficiency-consulting" company exclusively on the energy business, an industry she was learning a lot about in her day job. In fact, she set even more specific benchmarks for herself, deciding that she would take the leap to start her own business only after she signed her first client, and that she would open up her first office only after she signed up her third client, and so on.

To get her first client (the multinational company she was working for part-time), Berenice went right to the CEO and struck a deal: She would do the consulting work at one-sixth of the normal wage, but if she was successful in the assignment (and saved the client a certain amount of money in dealing with its vendors), she would get to tape and use a video testimonial of the CEO saying how amazing Berenice's work was and recommending it to others. It worked! To meet her promise and keep overhead low, Berenice spent the first year of her business working alone, and then for a while afterward with only one other consultant. Twelve years later, however, Berenice's business has more than 250 employees in six different offices throughout Brazil. Her clients include some of Brazil's largest corporations and a couple of Fortune 500 multinationals.

Berenice was able to achieve her grand entrepreneurial dream by staying "maniacally focused," as a business-school professor I know likes to put it. Having learned the hard way in her first business, Berenice forced herself to stay disciplined the second time around. Although her overall vision included working throughout Brazil across many different industry sectors, she started right at home in Rio (and even closer to home, by focusing her efforts on getting her former employer as a client!) and expanded to a new city or a new client type only when she was absolutely certain that she had mastered the previous plateau in her business.

A focused, disciplined approach is what set Berenice on the journey to creating one of the top independent corporate consultancies in Brazil. Focus is absolutely key and goes against the grain of most entrepreneurial minds (including Berenice's, at first). While currencies like money, courage, recognition, and victory stir us to think big and scale high mountains, successful execution begins with thinking small and learning how to scale to plateaus, rest, and then scale again. And this is where the business plan comes in. Berenice started out right the second time, by forcing

Focus In

Like Berenice, most successful modern entrepreneurs focused their original grand ideas down to a more refined concept, or started in something else altogether.

PERSON/COMPANY	ORIGINAL IDEA	REFINED, FOCUSED CONCEPT
David Packard and Bill Hewlett/Hewlett Packard	Machine tool monitoring systems, overall corporate information processing systems	Calculators
Howard Schultz/ Starbucks	Various retail, food, and live music venues	Coffee shops
John D. Rockefeller/ Standard Oil	Railroad and depot construction, fueling stations, and food distribution	Oil fields
Henry Ford/Ford Motor Company	Compact internal combusion engines for every type of industrial and commercial use	Cars

herself to limit the scope and focus of her business idea. But her real long-term success came from her ability to convert her focused idea into an operational plan, one with clear metrics and milestones.

I get to the all-important business plan momentarily. But first, before you move on, listen to the audio track corresponding to Chapter 4, "Inspiration and Focus," on the *Exercises and*

Visualizations CDs. One of the guided exercises will help you open your heart and mind to inspiration, based on your entrepreneurial currencies and your current life circumstances. Another exercise will help you refine your current entrepreneurial idea, focusing in on immediate areas of market-based implementation and development. Once you have gone through the audio tracks on the *Exercises and Visualizations* CDs (which will lead you to a Workbook exercise as well), refer to Business Plan Card 1, which will give you practical tips to identify and refine inspiration when it comes.

Step 2. Planning

The easiest way to raise the heart rate and elicit butterflies in the stomach of entrepreneurs is to ask for their business plan. I don't mean a loose-fitting description of their brilliant big idea. That's easy—every entrepreneur welcomes the opportunity for cocktail party talk about his or her business. The tough part is extracting a cogent, well-written plan on the business's intended development, complete with a study of customer demand, prospective competition, product development, and so on. A friend of mine writes entrepreneurial business plans of this kind for a living, through her own firm called Venture Architects. Having written hundreds of such plans over the years, she has a theory. Near the outset of an entrepreneurial project, the more "real" the entrepreneur's prospects for success—the more traction a project is already getting in the market, or the more innovative the product offering—the *less* likely there is to be a well-organized plan. This follows the rough logic many entrepreneurs like to use as an excuse when they haven't yet gotten their act together and written an organized business plan: "If I had the time to write a plan, I wouldn't have a really good new business (or new business *idea*) on my hands."

Certainly you need to focus on the business itself, not just produce fancy documents and presentations (witness my emphasis on focus and prioritization). Nevertheless, this line of reasoning functions basically as an excuse, and the logic is bunk. A small business may be able to *survive* at a subsistence level without a clear development plan, but it will never *progress* beyond the helter-skelter reality of a sole proprietorship or a small retail store or two if there isn't an organized business plan in place—one that helps an entrepreneur clearly articulate to himself or herself and others how it is he or she intends to get from point A in the business's development to point B. Even one-person operations run out of a living room must have a cogent plan if they intend to progress from serving one client to serving three, or to improve the quality of their services over time. Success doesn't happen by accident. Hence, my friend the business-plan writer's second rule of thumb: The more successful a business down the road, the

A Goal Without a Plan Is Just a Wish

The supreme example of this is the fly caught indoors. Eyeing a glass panel, it spends all its time frantically beating its body against the glass, determined to extricate itself. Although the fly has a clear, determined objective (getting outside) and is willing to expend enormous energy in pursuing its goal (so much so that it usually dies trying), it is clear that pausing in its frantic pursuit to plan a bit would yield considerably better results (observation of a nearby door ajar, or rediscovery of the hole in the screen through which it entered the house originally). As banal as this example may seem, take a careful, unvarnished look at your own behavior in professional (and perhaps personal) life. How many times have you behaved like the fly, beating yourself to exhaustion trying to achieve an objective that could have been reached calmly and relatively easily by other means? If you're similar to me and most other entrepreneurs and are being honest with yourself, you'll probably see that it happens often.

more likely it is in its development to have invested time and effort in disciplined planning. Although they're loath to admit it, the typical entrepreneurs tend to think that passion, drive, and stick-to-it-iveness can make up for a lack of planning; or, in slightly more acceptable jargon, being supremely "end-goal oriented" is the key to success. It's not. There's simply no substitute for rigorous planning.

Entrepreneurs tend to be impatient, passionate, and utterly determined. Those of us with primary currencies like courage, victory, and recognition tend to be even more emotionally geared than the entrepreneurial norm. Therefore it is critical that we always remain attentive to the risk of being the fanatic fly caught banging against a closed window. We'll never get out (achieve our entrepreneurial dreams) that way. We must take a breath, regroup, step back, and *plan*. Chuck Jones, the creator of Looney Tunes, put it best. "A fanatic is one who redoubles his effort when he has forgotten his aim," he said (paraphrasing the great philosopher George Santayana), when trying to explain the travails of Wile E. Coyote. Entrepreneurs must avoid the tendency to be the directionless fanatic.

What Is a Business Plan?

Okay, let's assume that I have convinced you of the importance of planning. But what does *planning* really mean? Is it having a really good to-do list, or a pretty slideshow done up for customers in Microsoft PowerPoint format? Is it having Monday morning organization meetings with the team, around a table of coffee and doughnuts? Should we obsess about having a single *document*, where the business's master plan is spelled out in black and white? How long does the document have to be? How many months or years ahead should it purport to cover? These are the questions that tie up many entrepreneurs in knots. The particularly knotted ones are those who have run their own businesses for many years already—the shop owner or the work-at-home graphic designer— but have never had a true business plan developed, and who come to the concept of the overriding importance of planning with a good degree of skepticism. "Why do I need a piece of paper that governs my business?" a small musical instruments retailer asked me recently. "I've never had one before, and we've been running this thing for twenty-four years." Unfortunately, the "thing" that she was referring to was a business in a great deal of financial peril, on the verge of foreclosure by its bank, and lacking in the basic tracking tools (spreadsheets, sales plans, etc.) even to *identify* the problems in the business, much less correct them.

Documents *are* important. Although a written plan cannot substitute for good communication among the entrepreneurial team, well-crafted sales presentations, or the passion and determination of a business owner, without a master business plan in written form it's hard for a business really to evolve. A written business plan is a reference document that an entrepreneur, partners, employees—even vendors, lenders, and investors—can turn to figure out what the business is going to be (in the case of a start-up business plan) or where the business is going (for a small business already off the ground), and measure whether things are on track. Therefore it's important that a business plan not only speak to the strategic goals of a business but also get into the nitty-gritty of sales milestones, product development milestones, employee expectations, office space planning, and so on. In the words of management guru Peter Drucker, "If you can't measure it, you can't improve it."

The Structure of the Business Plan

A good business plan must have the following seven components:

1. **Statement of Purpose:** A clearly stated explanation of the company's objective, from the perspective of the customer/marketplace. In a sense, finding your business's statement of purpose is a bit like discovering your business's currency. It's important not to mix up your business's currency and your *own* currency. "To make money," for example, might reflect your primary currency (you should go back to Chapter 1 if you haven't figured this out yet), but it does *not* count as an appropriate corporate statement of purpose. "To provide quality and affordable cleaning services to commercial and residential buildings in the Peoria area" would qualify. So would, "To bake the best chocolate-chip cookies in New England," or "To sell natural hair-care products online." A statement of purpose must be clear, descriptive of a particular product or service offering, and bound by at least one—and ideally two or more—of the following "value proposition" variables: geography, customer type, selling mechanism, price-point, or unique product/service attribute. When I started my first business, in college, my statement of purpose was, "To provide custom-imprinted caps and T-shirts to businesses and academic institutions in the Boston area." For easy tips on how to come up with (or discover) your business's (or business idea's) currency, see Business Plan Card 2.

2. **Market Background:** A concise review of the current market for the particular product or service being offered by the company. This cannot be conjecture, e.g., "The market for a new architecture firm in Texarkana is extremely strong, because there is

a tremendous amount of new construction going on." Cut out *everything* in the market background section that is not completely fact based, and delve into detail. How many people live in Texarkana? Why is this the only local market of interest? What about the neighboring towns or counties? How many new buildings have gone up in the last few years? How did they split among residential, industrial, and commercial construction? Would the architecture firm being presented in the business plan focus only on so-called new starts, or would it also work on remodeling projects? How much activity in each of these categories has been seen in Texarkana (and the surrounding market) recently? Do local consumers of architectural plans display a proclivity toward certain styles or projects? And so forth. At each level of question, go one level deeper, until there is no more detail to glean. It takes a great deal of research and patience.

Entrepreneurs often have a difficult time with the market background section of the business plan. They tend to think they have a mastery over a certain subject matter and assume they don't have to do the deeper digging for information. Or they get bored with the level of detail required and say to themselves, "It doesn't matter, anyway. Who's going to know the difference?" This cutting corners and failure to do a full market background results in the second-most-common killer (the most common being lack of focus) of entrepreneurial projects: a lack of sufficient research into the market opportunity being addressed. I have seen too many clients who spend months (even years) developing a "unique" new product, only to discover that there are three other producers in (pick your region) offering it already whom they could have gone to as a reseller; or who spend too little time really learning about their competition and customer demographics, and end up offering inappropriate or ill-conceived services to their addressable market (opening up a gym next door to Gold's new location, or providing "cheap" college prep tutoring services at nearly twice Kaplan's rate). Often, these missteps are entirely avoidable by doing a little more research (the gym might be a hip new format, just in need of a different location, or the tutoring business might need to be pitched for its personalized, one-on-one appeal instead of its discount prices). For easy tips on how to research your market effectively and successfully, refer to Business Plan Cards 3 and 4.

3. **Product/Service Offering Description:** For many entrepreneurs, this is the easiest section of the business plan. This is where you get to carry on about the virtues of your cute little retail store, or the world-beating cuisine at the restaurant you intend to open. The offering description section forces you to think carefully about what makes your particular idea or business special—the unique attributes that will make the product a must-have, or the carefully thought out approach to marketing that will pull clients away from the competition. Don't succumb to thinking that your new business has to create an innovative new product or service; it can just as likely be a new way of thinking about marketing, store location, or an enhanced level of customer service. "If you want to identify a successful start-up," says Bill Sahlman, professor of entrepreneurship at Harvard Business School, "look for better execution of an old idea before you look for a truly new idea." Keeping this in mind, make the offering description section clear and detailed. Write it as much for yourself (to keep your eyes on what your competitive advantage is going to be in the market) as for others

(employees, customers, investors, and so on) who may ultimately read your business plan. For easy tips on how to distill your company's offering attributes into a concise description, refer to Business Plan Card 5.

4. **Team Overview:** Like the free-throw shot in basketball, this is the most seemingly rote part of your business plan, yet it's the one that's easiest to screw up. Even one-person businesses need a team overview. Your entrepreneurial project is nothing without its people (or person). In my seminars, many entrepreneurs get to the team overview section of the business plan and think they can go on autopilot. "How many times can I write my own bio?" you might think to yourself. Or "This is simple: I just need to get together a brief description of me, my partner, and the sales guy." Not so. This section is not just for presentation purposes. Your team overview should include *all* the members of your core entrepreneurial team, including yourself, of course, your senior partners and employees, and your lawyer, accountant, business advisers—even your first customer if the learning you're getting from your first assignment or sale is critical to the way you are going to develop your product. If you have a board of directors established (see Observation Cards 41–44), you should also include brief bios of those board members in your team overview section.

Think of your team as a community, not as the recipients of payroll. Include in your business plan a description of each team member and also include what you expect to get from each member of the team (support on getting particular customers signed up, or guidance on how to set up your storefront shelves). Get as specific as you can in these expectations, being completely honest with yourself as to where responsibility and accountability lie in each and every aspect of your business. Finally, put together a sample organizational chart, showing who's responsible for what and who reports to whom. If you're a one-person company, you should still create an organizational chart and include the individuals whom you work with on your business but whom you don't pay directly as employees (your lawyer, your office supplies source). You might need to play around with the structure and consider several variations.

Take mapping out your business's structure seriously. This is your chance to get it all out on paper, so you have a visual tool for the future. As your business changes over time, I encourage you to update your team overview section and refresh your organizational chart. For a couple of sample organizational charts (including one designed for a sole proprietorship) and tips on mapping out your entrepreneurial "team," see Business Plan Cards 6 and 7.

5. Execution: In the next section of this chapter, I address the implementation of your business plan in more detail. For the moment, however, the execution section of your written document is a good place to start to wrestle with the nettlesome details of how you're going to get from point A (an idea in your garage, or one retail location on a side street) to point B (office space and a desk, or three stores on Main Street in three different towns). This is by far the most difficult part of every business plan. It is where you take your inspirational idea and bring it down to earth in a chronological, bread-and-butter kind of way. If you want a visual representation of the execution section of your business plan, think about those classic old Dunkin' Donuts TV ads. The disheveled doughnut shop proprietor would get out of bed, jarred awake by his alarm clock before the sun had even come out. "It's time to make the doughnuts," he would say, half groaning, staring glassy-eyed into the camera. Then the scene would pan to the morning rush-hour crowd pouring into the same proprietor's Dunkin' Donuts location. Now he would have a bright look on his face, the sun would be coming in the windows, and he'd be serving hot, fresh pastries to his smiling clientele.

Executing entrepreneurial plans in the real world, as anybody who's gone through it will tell you, is a bit like "making the doughnuts" every morning. There's always the rush of success and pride of authorship in providing the final product, but leading up to that is grueling, repetitive work that requires undying commitment and a certain tolerance for pain. Now imagine if the doughnut guy of those advertisements decided he wanted to serve the hottest and freshest doughnuts in the land but didn't think ahead enough to wake up early and make the batter. It's obvious he would fail. Yet many entrepreneurs make the same stupid mistake. The devil's in the details, and the execution section of your business plan is where you address the majority of these details: getting the licenses required by the state you live in to perform certain services or open a certain kind of establishment, the time it takes to get a certain product on the shelf in anticipation of a heavy buying season, the background checks you need to do on prospective employees.

The execution section of your business plan is where my previous warnings about tethering your camel come into play. It is the domain of the mundane, where you need to think about and write down production schedules, delivery processes, and customer service protocols. It may not be what drew you to an entrepreneurial lifestyle in the first place, but it is what will allow you to be successful at it. In combination with the financial model (described below), the execution section of your business plan will set out the operational/financial milestones that you will strive for as your business evolves. For all-important guidance on how to sketch the nitty-gritty processes and procedures of your business, see Business Plan Cards 8–10.

6. **Risk Factors:** For the average entrepreneur, the risk factors section of a business plan raises hackles and causes discomfort. This is where you need to think of all the things that could go wrong in your business, from a misreading of demand for a product in the market, to hiring the wrong store manager, to screwing up your first client project. This is scary territory. It's where you step back and poke holes in your business plan as a whole and assume the worst. Risk factors include the lawsuit you never want to face, the late delivery of inventory you live in fear of, and the late-paying client who could completely throw off your cash flow. It is the land of unforeseen problems and stupid decisions. To write a really useful risk factors section, you must temporarily resist the entrepreneur's proclivity toward positive thinking and let your fears and doubts be exposed. What would happen if your restaurant didn't get its liquor license? Or if your distributor suddenly refused to carry your product anymore? What if an unexpected tax payment came due next quarter? Or one of your partners quit tomorrow and sued over intellectual property rights? These are the horrible realities that—while unlikely and to be avoided at all costs—must be planned for.

While it is prudent when raising money (particularly from a legal liability perspective) to list out as many risk factors as you can come up with, in general you should prioritize a discussion of those risks with the highest probability of materializing. The risk factors section of your business plan must not use vague and sugar-coated terms that lawyers put in public company prospectuses (with titles like "market uncertainty" or "potential loss of key clientele"), but should reflect the raw and harsh reality of your small business or sole proprietorship. Working with hundreds of small business owners and aspiring entrepreneurs, I have observed a clear pattern over time: The less dewy-eyed and more brutally realistic an entrepreneur is about the downside and risks, the less likely he or she is ever to confront the problems contemplated or to be bowled over by the problems if and when they do arise. While this is not a particularly profound observation, it is one that most optimistically inclined entrepreneurs ignore. For tips on capturing all the common risks and pitfalls associated with entrepreneurial projects, see Chapter 2 on entrepreneurial Achilles' heels and Business Plan Cards 11–12.

7. **Financial Model in Spreadsheet Form:** This final part of your business plan is considered fun by some entrepreneurs but overwhelming and confusing by most: your operating plan converted into spreadsheet form. What does this mean? It's where you take your business's previous financial performance (if you already have a business up and running) and put it on paper, in numerical form, next to the financial performance you predict for your business in the future. You can do this using one of several computer spreadsheet programs, including Excel or Lotus. If you don't know how to manage a spreadsheet program yourself, find someone who does. Your accountant can help you with this exercise, or a financial planner who specializes in small businesses. If you're a numbers person, you've probably already gone through the exercise of doing financial modeling for your business or business idea; if you aren't, this part of your business plan is

going to take some courage and hard work, but you've absolutely got to do it. No business has ever succeeded for more than a brief period of time without good financial planning and budgeting.

The financial model section of the business plan should mesh with the execution section. For example, if you recognize in your execution section that you are going to need to invest in new equipment at the beginning of next year, your financial model section must show how this upcoming expense flows through your financial statements. A solid financial model section of your business plan goes back at least two years into the past (in cases where operating history exists), and out at least two years into the future. The financial model will at least include cash-flow projections (including sources and uses of cash), working capital needs assessment, and balance sheet projections. Line items on all of these must be broken down at the most detailed level possible, including things like salaries and benefits for individual employees (as opposed to lumping it together in a group "employee expenses" line) and the cost of every input you can think of in the business (rent, utilities, marketing materials, office supplies, insurance, inventory purchases, and so on). Together with your execution section, the financial model in your business plan will set out the operational and financial milestones that you will strive for as your business evolves. For further advice on developing your financial model, and for sample financial models, see Business Plan Cards 13–16.

The detailed business plan is an oft-neglected step in entrepreneurial development. It is just as critical to the successful evolution of an established small business as it is to the initial push of a start-up, although people usually only associate business plans with start-ups. Don't skimp on your business plan. Make it your organizing document; it keeps you focused, enables you to judge your progress as a business, and helps you anticipate pitfalls along the way. Keep it with you at all times and mark it up with abandon. Use the Business Plan Cards and your Workbook notes on this section to develop your own business plan.

Step 3. Implementation and Adjustment

You now have the essential tools for entrepreneurial success. You know your primary currency; you have been versed on the dangers of your Achilles' heels; and you have been steeped in the practical grounding of a successful entrepreneurial plan. In this chapter in particular, you have studied the need for focus, as you refine your original entrepreneurial idea into a clear business plan. So what's left? *Implementing* the business plan. The keys to success in this respect are threefold: two are the same themes that have already threaded themselves throughout this kit—focus and discipline; the third theme is somewhat new and perhaps the most enigmatic—flexibility. Consider the following examples, which illustrate the importance of having a focused business plan, *and* the ability to constantly re-evaluate and adapt that plan to changing realities.

SmileAlert

Dr. Levy, a successful dentist with a thriving high-end practice in Manhattan, did all the right things in setting up SmileAlert—which was in effect his second entrepreneurial venture (his first being his dental practice). SmileAlert was conceived as the vehicle for Dr. Levy to market and sell a new tooth-whitening concoction he had patented. As with many entrepreneurial projects, it began organically, with Dr. Levy testing it out on a few patients and getting positive responses. Soon, however, he realized that his new product had the potential to be sold to a wider customer base than his patients, and he began to explore how to develop SmileAlert as a separate enterprise.

Here is where Dr. Levy took the right steps. He started by sketching out his goals for the product and the business, and candidly reflecting on his own entrepreneurial currencies: health (primary) and money (secondary). Knowing that he wanted to keep a balanced lifestyle (and his regular practice was already quite busy) and generate excellent financial returns on his new pet project, he decided to find other people to run the day-to-day operations of SmileAlert. He also had the sense to give these new managers some free rein in developing their own approach to the business. He set them up with a small office in midtown Manhattan and encouraged them to develop a true business plan—complete with a statement of purpose ("To sell easy-to-use tooth-whitening products that are affordable, safe, and self-applied"), market background, product overview, implementation section, risk factors, and financial model. Soon, the revenues from SmileAlert were eclipsing those of Dr. Levy's traditional business.

Now Dr. Levy put the icing on the cake of his own entrepreneurial success: He had the *flexibility* to recognize the changes that were taking place in the landscape of his professional life and adjusted his schedule so he could spend more of his time engaged in ongoing product improvement, marketing, and public relations for the SmileAlert business. But keeping his underlying currencies in mind, he was smart enough not to take over the day-to-day operation of SmileAlert and avoided the forgetfulness (or self-delusion) trap that often ensnares the entrepreneur experiencing heady growth in his business. Dr. Levy perfectly balanced (a) an original focus on his core dentistry business and his motivating currencies, (b) rigorous planning on the new SmileAlert business, and (c) smooth adaptation/adjustment to the emerging realities of a growing secondary business.

Rising Tide Studios

If the example of SmileAlert seems too good to be true, consider the rocky road of adaptation represented by Rising Tide Studios, LLC. Rising Tide was founded in 1996 by a young entrepreneur named Jason Calacanis.* Jason's parents had long struggled to make ends meet as the proprietors of a small Greek restaurant in Bay Ridge, Brooklyn. Jason, who worked in the restaurant from the age of fourteen onward, finally finished his studies at Fordham University in 1991 after several periods out of school saving up tuition by fixing electronic equipment. Always a dreamer, Jason had grown up addicted to science fiction. After school, Jason wedged his way into the high-octane professional world of Apple Computer and Adobe, finding work as a consultant at each firm in the early 1990s.

Eventually, his love of prose and the borderless possibilities of technology and science combined in Rising Tide Studios: an after-hours entrepreneurial venture selling a homemade, foldout newsletter reporting heard-on-the-street developments in the technology industry in the New York area. He called it the *Silicon Alley Reporter*, and the name stuck. Unsurprisingly, Jason's primary currency is recognition, and his little newsletter received so much recognition that it helped put the moniker "Silicon Alley" on New York's buzzing technology-steeped Flatiron District. Without too much planning, Jason continued to piece together *Silicon Alley Reporter (SAR)* each month, often drawing on credit cards to pay the printer or his graphic designer. Soon, however, the technology

*Mr. Calacanis' name appears with his permission.

boom swept the country, and Jason's newsletter became the hottest thing around. By 1998, Jason had long ago quit his day job, and *SAR* was a 100-page glossy publication with advertisements from car companies, brokerage houses, and haute couture designers, all peddling to an affluent young readership base. Jason felt like he was on top of the world and raised millions of dollars in outside financing. Jason began to develop a longer-term, documented business plan, and the discipline of the exercise helped: He quickly realized that the market size for a regional trade publication was simply too limited to justify his predictions for growth and the intended uses for the money he had raised.

Jason's first step into the world of business planning was opportune and critically timed. He also deserves credit for actually heeding the results of his objective business plan development and beginning to practically adjust the direction of his venture. By late 1999, Jason was generating more of his revenues from conferences, trade shows, and roundtable discussions than he was with the original publication. Although he sensed that the boom in dot-com advertising would end, it was unlikely that people in the technology industry would stop getting together to exchange ideas, contacts, and business information. Yet even in this arena, Jason trod carefully, and when the crash in the stock market finally hit its third dip in November 2000, he had evolved his business sufficiently to include a third revenue stream: a database with the contact information of nearly all the senior company and venture capital executives in the technology business nationwide. He had begun putting together this unique database a couple of years before, as he was doing the market background work for his business plan, culling the data from his subscriber lists and, later, from his attendee lists at *SAR*-sponsored conferences and trade shows.

This third revenue stream literally saved Jason's business. Print magazine advertising in the technology sector fell off a cliff in early 2001 (hence the demise of publications like *Red Herring, Industry Standard, Internet World*, and others), and even the technology conference and trade show businesses were moribund. However, in a more sparse journalistic environment, Jason's database (and his ensuing daily "email blast" on current events in the industry) became a hot and necessary commodity. Jason quickly set about developing a new business plan for *SAR*, which he renamed *Venture Reporter* to stay away from the dot-com stigma. Because Jason was a stickler for planning ahead, and approached his entrepreneurial venture with the humility of someone who is constantly watching market changes and his customers' evolving tastes and needs, he was able to adjust and survive one of the most turbulent economic periods in decades. In fact, in early 2003, I helped Jason make a final adjustment, when he sold Rising Tide Studios to a strategic acquirer and took on a senior management role in the acquiring entity—a company nearly fifty times the size of his small enterprise.

SmileAlert and Rising Tide Studios are two of the many entrepreneurial adventures I have observed over the years where adaptiveness and flexibility have combined with planning and foresight to predicate success. The three-step developmental journey—from original inspiration to focus, then planning and, finally, adjustment—is evident in the experience of nearly every successful entrepreneur I have come across. I have also experienced the need for adjustment in business planning the hard way.

> "Planning is invaluable: A plan that cannot be changed is worthless."
> —Sir Winston Churchill

In my second business, one of my venture capital backers told me, "You have to know your plan well enough to know what you have to change when things go wrong." He could not have been more right. While building govWorks, I stuck to our original idea of selling parking ticket and real estate tax financial-processing services directly to citizens, even though the market was clearly telling us to sell these services and software to the cities and counties themselves, so they could implement it for their citizens' use. This delay in implementation cost time and money that might have saved the company down the road. As entrepreneurs, we must learn to see our business plan as a directive document to follow but also as an experimental plan to break. By following it, we stay on track to success. By breaking it and carefully observing the results, we measure what works and what doesn't, and open ourselves to necessary changes. Of course, we have to be careful not to go too far too fast. Adjustments need to be incremental enough for us to test them as we go. Consider the example of a company I will call SuperTrade.

SuperTrade

SuperTrade was a small broker-dealer started in 1998. The founder, Gloria, was a longtime employee in a large stock-trading service we'll call Clearwave. Gloria, who had worked in the securities-trading field for many years, worked her way through the ranks of Clearwave, where by the late 1990s she was running the Latin American stock-trading business. Yet what Gloria really wanted to do was run her own broker-dealer. Knowing that the field was extremely competitive, and fearing obliteration by the legion of well-funded start-ups in the industry, Gloria came up with a deceptively simple yet brilliant plan. As an immigrant from Spain to the United States, Gloria had always been encouraged to work with the Spanish-language areas of Clearwave's business, and she had developed strong relationships with Latin America–based money management firms as well as several influential U.S.-based Hispanic fund managers. She knew that if she went out on her own, she could probably attract some of the Hispanic-run funds and Latin America–based funds to do business with her—as long as she could assure them that her stock-trading services were at least as good as Clearwave's services. She also figured that by campaigning to get the business for minority set-asides at the public pension funds (by state law, teachers' retirement funds, police and firefighters' funds, and other such pension plans have to send a certain percentage of their trading business to minority-owned firms), she could probably get a small slice of a big trading pie.

Gloria registered SuperTrade as a minority-owned business and developed her business plan exclusively oriented toward the Latin American, Hispanic, and large pension fund minority set-asides. She also added a final touch of sheer brilliance: She went to Clearwave's biggest competitor and got them to invest in her new company and commit to managing all the back-office trading! This meant that Gloria could go to all of her former clients at Clearwave (and others to boot) and legitimately claim that the stock-trading execution services that they would get with her new firm would be just as good as if they were dealing with Clearwave or its prime competitor. Gloria had done intensive market research and planning, and stayed true to her client acquisition plan, focusing exclusively on her chosen markets. SuperTrade grew quickly and was profitable on more than $6.4 million of revenue in only its second year.

But it was near the beginning of her third year in business that Gloria sowed the seeds of her own downfall. Her primary currency had always been courage, and she fell prey to its most common weakness: the loss of focus and assumption of excessive risk that comes from the courage-driven entrepreneur's addictlike search for the next "big thing"—the next mountain to climb, the next adrenaline rush. Instead of remaining focused on her business plan and continuing to sell in a disciplined manner to the hundreds of Latin American money managers and thousands of U.S.-based pension funds with minority set-aside programs (Gloria's business plan itself estimated the size of the addressable market to be in excess of $500 million annually, of which she had captured only about 1 percent in her first two years), Gloria began to envision SuperTrade becoming a full-service trading firm—complete with company research reports and stock recommendations. She strayed from her core competency of executing trades just as well as anybody else in the market ("best execution," as it is called).

Even though Gloria had a sales and client acquisition advantage owing to SuperTrade's Hispanic angle, she felt the need to innovate for innovation's sake (remember Professor Sahlman's admonition about it being better to have an old idea well executed than a new idea). She began to sink tens, then hundreds of thousands of dollars into hiring high-flying stock market research professionals and got fancy new office space. She spent less and less time in the field selling and paid more attention to her new pet project internally. It didn't take long for it to all come crashing down. By its fourth year, SuperTrade's revenues had dropped to under $2 million, it was losing money, and it was temporarily suspended from doing business by the National Association of Securities Dealers for falling below required net capitalization ratios.

Gloria did not heed the feedback her market was so clearly giving her—that her original business plan was working!—and went headlong into major changes to her business model when no real adjustment was called for. Furthermore, she failed to test these changes carefully as she went. Gloria lost focus, ignored her original planning, and adapted her business model to wishful thinking as opposed to market feedback.

Gloria's tale of caution with SuperTrade is not uncommon in its basic outlines. While most small and start-up businesses fail due to lack of initial focus and planning, a fair share of entrepreneurial ventures fail after the fact because they stop dutifully implementing their business plan, especially when success starts to seem easy. Implementation of a business plan is a balancing act—a delicate combination of following the letter of the law, so to speak, while being open to and aware of the market feedback that contradicts the original plan—and having the strength of conviction to make the necessary adjustments.

As discussed above, the right way to think of a business plan is as both a directive and an experimental document: It's there to guide you in what to do and provide the benchmark to help you decide what *not* to do. The real danger comes not from making changes to your business plan (SmileAlert and Rising Tide Studios both made adjustments) but from not doing the proper research up front and ignoring market feedback and lessons learned along the way. The key is to stay focused and *aware*, constantly watching out for the classic entrepreneurial traps as your business evolves. For more advice on specific topics you are likely to confront in the implementation of your plan, consult Business Plan Cards 17–40 and refer to the corresponding Workbook exercises.

Chapter 4 Conclusion

From the beginning of this lesson plan, I have emphasized the importance of self-awareness—whether with respect to your own internal drivers, your potential Achilles' heels, or the practical challenges of business planning and growth. No guidebook or lesson plan will make you immune to mistakes along the perilous path of entrepreneurship. But by regularly using exercises like the Moment of Solidity in Chapter 1, the Hanuman Stance in Chapter 2, and the Observer in Chapter 3, you will cultivate self-knowledge and give yourself the mental and emotional space to harness your strengths and minimize your vulnerabilities.

In this chapter you explored the importance of focus in developing your business—from refining your original idea, to developing a business plan, to implementing and adjusting that business plan in the market. In a sense, you got more "practical" in Chapters 3 and 4, and the Observation Cards and Business Plan Cards provided additional practical input on the everyday challenges of entrepreneurial planning and implementation. You must remember, however, that the heart of entrepreneurship is where the abstract—the spiritual—and the practical *meet*. Knowing your currency without knowing how to draft a business plan is relatively useless knowledge. By the same token, knowing how to build your business's financial model without recognizing the ensnarements of the money trap is equally fruitless.

Before turning to the next chapter, listen to the final audio track for Chapter 4 on the *Exercises and Visualizations* CDs. Have your Workbook ready as well, since you will be asked to pinpoint the places where your currencies and Achilles' heels are likely to come to bear in implementing your business plan.

Chapter 5: Enjoy the Journey

Embracing Success and Failure

The market for books that claim to offer a silver bullet for business success is endless. From Frederick W. Taylor's *Shop Management* (1903) to Spencer Johnson's *Who Moved My Cheese?* (1998), each attempts to reduce success to its essential elements, both psychological and organizational, and then lay these elements out on the table. What I find most interesting about this endless stream of books is the way they take the definition of their goal—success in business—for granted. What does "success" mean, anyway? Judging by the most celebrated of the business-publishing field—from Alfred P. Sloan's *My Years with General Motors* (1964) to Jack Welch's *Straight from the Gut* (2001)—success is generally associated with making a lot of money and getting a lot of recognition for how you made a lot of money. This seems reasonable in a capitalist society and, at first blush, a good enough definition.

But the picture gets fuzzier as we get closer to the facts. How long does "success" have to last for it to be worthy of study and emulation? For example, Henri Fayol's classic study on top-down management, *General and Industrial Management* (1916), held up at the time as the tome that would "put an end to the need for business literature," went out of style by the Great Depression. International Telephone & Telegraph (ITT), the lion of the corporate jungle in the 1960s and early '70s and the subject of numerous publishing laurels during that time, was considered a degenerate corporate dinosaur by the late 1970s and became the subject of one of the most searing indictments of a business with the release of Robert Sobel's *ITT: The Management of Opportunity* in

1982. Perhaps the most startling example of the business "success" fad are the nearly twenty best-selling titles on the dot-com boom (from *Blown to Bits* to *First, Break All the Rules*), some of which idolized business models and entrepreneurs who had gone bankrupt by the time the books idolizing them had hit the bookshelves. Today's heroes are tomorrow's goats, to which the executives at erstwhile firms like Global Crossing, Enron, and Worldcom would attest.

Redefining Success

Some professional students of business, perturbed at the rapidity with which brilliant ideas become bunk and brilliant companies go out of business, have taken a more cautious approach. Jim Collins, for example, defines success as a business's ability to *evolve* and traverse developmental hurdles. Nancy Koehn, the Harvard professor I mentioned earlier, refuses to put an entrepreneur or a company on a pedestal until the entrepreneurial project has proved profitable and growing for decades. While these are interesting solutions to the dilemma of "picking the wrong horse," so to speak, there is a more specific, daring, and—I believe—more accurate definition of entrepreneurial success: *to enjoy the journey.*

This phrase seems to elicit both deep-seated recognition and deep-seated discomfort in the typical reader. On the one hand, we all know deep down that the point of everything we do on this earth is to be happy. Almost all the entrepreneurs I have worked with over the years use words like "fulfillment," "destiny," or "joy" when describing why they got into the entrepreneurial game in the first place. Any levelheaded businessperson has to acknowledge that going down the entrepreneurial path is, statistically speaking, a poor choice if one's goal is to ensure the accumulation of serious wealth. After all, seven out of ten businesses fail in their first three years, and nine out of ten fail in their first ten years.

Given this harsh reality, a successful entrepreneur is one who enjoys the ride fully, its dramatic ups and even its downs. Yet there is a part of all of us that refuses to accept the idea that we can actually *enjoy* anything other than material success in business. I call this tendency the "fairy tale complex." It's the feeling that if we do not make gobs of money, or receive lots of public accolades and praise, how can we possibly let ourselves be happy? This doubting inner voice worries that the only happy life is the fairy tale life, complete with wealth, health, and a problem-free, hassle-free existence, that being happy with anything less is complacent, wrong. . .un-American. It's the part of us that unconsciously sides with the trend-loving business media, lionizing the hot tycoon or business fad of the moment, and sweeping yesterday's failures and embarrassments under the rug.

If this kit accomplishes nothing else for you, I hope it may prevent you from being caught up in the fairy tale complex and from being embarrassed by failure. Every truly successful entrepreneur I have ever met (including a nice smattering of billionaires) has learned the importance of *embracing* his or her failures. Openly admitting to, studying, and learning from your failures is one of the most difficult things to do in business. It is tougher than the most grueling client presentation you've ever done and more challenging than the leanest financial moment you've experienced. It is the epitome of my central theme: truly *know yourself,* weaknesses and all. Embracing your own experience of failure as an entrepreneur opens the gates to personal transformation, future material successes, and your experience of the greatest success of all: peace and happiness on your entrepreneurial journey.

Where to Find the Secret to a Happy Life

There is a Native American story about how God went about deciding where to hide the Secret to a Happy Life from humans. God gathered together his animal advisers. "Where shall I put it?" he asked the Eagle.

The Eagle answered, "I shall hide it at the top of the highest mountain. Man will never find it there."

God considered this and decided against it. "One day, Man will go there," he said. Next, he asked the Clam. "Where shall I put it, little Clam?"

"I will hide it at the bottom of the deepest ocean," the Clam answered.

This seemed like a better idea, but the Lord hesitated again. "Man will go there too someday," he said after some thought.

Then, the wise Owl stepped forward. "Though I regretfully cannot take it there myself," he intoned, "perhaps you ought to hide the secret on the moon."

After considering this, God finally came to the same conclusion as before: "No. There, too, Man shall go."

After some period of reflection, the humble Opossum came forward. "Perhaps," he said, so softly that he could barely be heard, "the secret should be hidden in the heart of Man." There was an awed silence among the animals.

Finally, the Lord spoke: "Yes, cunning Opossum, that will be the last place Man will look."

Despite its simplicity, the moral of the story is proved true every day in my professional practice. I work with entrepreneurs from around the country and the world, of different ages, in different industries, and with wildly varying degrees of wealth. Day in and day out, I observe that the most enduring "successes" are not necessarily those with the largest bank accounts or the biggest businesses; they are the ones who thoroughly enjoy the entrepreneurial adventure and know that their happiness springs from within themselves. Because almost every entrepreneurial path involves numerous scrapes and falls, they are also the ones who have embraced their experiences of failure along the way and used failure's lessons both to reduce their tendency to make future mistakes and to put things into perspective so that they can more fully enjoy their outward successes.

The Power of Failure

Despite the well-known curative powers of failure, most first-time entrepreneurs are embarrassed to admit critical mistakes or failure. (The more seasoned entrepreneurs and investors are more likely to see the value of their experiences.) When I lead seminars for CEOs and business owners, I usually start with a simple exercise. I ask everyone to close his or her eyes—to encourage concentration, but also to avoid having people see what their neighbor is doing. Then I ask the participants to raise their hand if they are currently experiencing what they would personally define as a "crisis" in their business. I usually have to remind people there is no cheating tolerated when it comes to keeping their eyes closed (entrepreneurs are notoriously poor at following the rules!). On average, about two thirds of the hands go up in answer to the question on crisis. (I believe that closer to 90 percent of the hands would go up if people were totally assured of the confidentiality of the situation, since the participants are frequently sitting near other business owners and managers whom they know and are nervous that word will get out in their local business community.)

The second question follows from the first (and I ask everyone still to keep his or her eyes closed): How many of you have experienced failure—really painful, abject failure—at some point on your entrepreneurial path? I usually add that failure need not entail actually going out of business or going bankrupt, but should nonetheless mean "hitting the wall" somehow—whether it's having to downsize significantly, shut down stores, go through a painful personal or professional partnership breakup as a result of the business, and so on. In answer to this question, nearly all the hands go up.

In business management, crisis is universal. In entrepreneurship, failure is inevitable. There is no shame in admitting to these things, and if you're thinking to yourself, "What is this guy talking about? I haven't experienced real crisis or failure," or "I want to skip this pathetic stuff about tripping and failing," then one of two things is going on for you. Either you have never really stretched yourself or gone beyond your comfort zone as an entrepreneur, or you are in denial. Failure is so intrinsic to entrepreneurship that I dare say you are doing something *wrong* if you are not experiencing it with reasonable frequency; you are probably not testing the edges of your ability or the frontiers of your entrepreneurial idea. The key is to test these boundaries, and risk limited failure, without putting your whole business at risk, or jeopardizing your livelihood. If you are in a retail business, it can mean introducing new products that might not work but if successful would help keep your inventory fresh and current with customer tastes. If you are in a service business, it can mean experimenting with training on new techniques, trying new approaches to customers, or bringing new partners into the business. Many, if not most, innovations in your business will fail (including, perhaps, the very first leap out of the starting gate). But if you anticipate setbacks and busted plans—"manage for failure"—you will be able to navigate these trials.

Watch for what works and what doesn't in your business, so that you can learn from the failures—large and small—and improve your business (as well as your own attitude and self-knowledge) each step of the way. Learn to see your missteps as blessings. The painter Monet was once asked which of his many masterpieces was his favorite work. "I cherish my failures most of all," he said, to the shock of the crowd. He was said to have surrounded himself at his studio with his ugliest creations, half-filled canvases, and out-of-proportion vistas, so as to remind himself constantly of what *not* to do.

Famous Ups and Downs

Entrepreneur	Earlier Business Experiences	Eventual Peak
Walt Disney	Newspaper delivery boy, newspaper cartoonist, cheated out of first few years' of work by cartoon distributor	Founder of the Walt Disney Co.
Jimmy Goldsmith	Underground gambling parlor, generic pharmaceutical products, Alka-Seltzer salesman, insolvency (three times), single father	Billionaire, owner of Diamond International, Crown Zellerbach, and Grand Union Supermarkets
Mary Kay	Single mother, door-to-door saleswoman of basic home products, insolvency, grandmother by the time she founded her first business	Founder/CEO of Mary Kay Cosmetics
Ray Kroc	Paper cup salesman, jazz piano player, real estate broker, milkshake mixer, salesman	Founder/CEO of McDonald's Corporation
Tom Monaghan	Went bankrupt twice, lost control of his first pizza company, was sued for trademark violations	Founder of Domino's Pizza

The greatest creators—writers, artists, entrepreneurs—all echo this sentiment of appreciation for their creative and intellectual misfirings. Picasso is said to have avoided going to bed until he botched up some project or another (otherwise he didn't feel he had the appropriate reference point for inspiration when it came). Bill Gates evangelizes the value of failure to his development staff all the time: Progress, he says, is made only by becoming obsessed with what *doesn't* work. The Beatles used to carry around with them their most hated recordings, to remind themselves how they *shouldn't* sound.

Whether by virtue of concrete lessons learned from specific failed business initiatives, or by dint of the fire in the belly stoked by a previous bankruptcy or business humiliation, many of the world's most successful entrepreneurs attribute their success, in part, to their failure. Admittedly, having this attitude toward one's missteps in life is much easier said than done. We would all like to have faith in the old bromides that "things happen for a reason" or "what doesn't kill us makes us stronger." But deep down most of us wonder if these aren't just rationalizations we use so we don't feel like total losers when things go bad. That's what I used to think—that is, until I experienced my first big, complete, abject failure. . . and its unexpected aftermath.

My Own Failure

I started my second business in late 1998, as the dot-com bubble was expanding. The original statement of purpose for the business was "to allow people to pay for their parking electronically—either on the phone or via the Internet." The concept seemed simple, but it required a great deal of innovation on a couple of major fronts. We had to get entrenched local governmental authorities (mostly parking violation bureaus, municipal finance officials, and police departments) to accept the idea that payment of violations could be made by any means other than the mail. We also had to develop the financial software (actually, "middleware," as it was called) to make the transfer of money from people's bank accounts or credit cards to the somewhat Byzantine back-end financial systems used by local government. The original name of the business was Public Data Systems, a label that accurately reflected the somewhat mundane and detail-intensive tasks required to make the business successful.

For the first nine months of the business, I maintained a disciplined approach, spending hundreds of hours on the business plan and the product development process, while listening to the input of former municipal officials whom we had sought out for advice on the fledgling business. During this period, we watched every nickel, anticipating that our first big project implementation (and paycheck from a client) wasn't likely to occur for quite a while, given the complexity of the system we had to develop and the slowness of government agencies in reaching a purchasing decision and actually paying for anything.

The discipline of our planning, our cost-consciousness in spending, and the open-mindedness of our approach (we adjusted our initial software product several times near the start, in response to the feedback we received from the retired government officials we had approached) paid off: In the summer of 1999, we landed our first major client (Springfield, Massachusetts); soon after, East Hartford, Connecticut, signed on; and soon even New York City expressed an interest in testing our system. In response to this positive market feedback and growing momentum, we raised more than $19 million of venture capital in the fall of 1999. I felt like I was on top of the world.

But it was at the height of our initial success that I began to sow the seeds of my own destruction. Over time, I have realized that my secondary currency is recognition, and the dangerous side of recognition (succumbing to the ego boost that the attention the business was getting would give me, or becoming more interested in the accolades we were getting from government officials than in the prospective profitability of the product) began to take hold. I began to "believe my own hype," as a former employee would put it years later, and I lost touch with the penny-pinching and agonizingly detailed planning of our initial stages of development.

Over the next eighteen months, I fell into nearly every trap described in this book and got to know every Achilles' heel. I became disconnected from the positive elements of my currencies—courage and recognition—and became addicted to the derring-do and renown that came from the "bigness" of what I thought we were building. Now renamed the sexier-sounding govWorks, my business's statement of purpose changed to the grander—and ultimately unrealistic—"to fundamentally change the way citizens interact with their local government." Having lost my moorings, I fell hook, line, and sinker for the forgetfulness (or self-delusion) trap. Trying to satisfy the voracious appetites of the venture capitalists, the media, and my own ego, I rushed the product to market, cutting corners in the process and ignoring a lot of valuable feedback still coming from our advisory board. Thus, I also succumbed to the expediency trap. The money trap quickly became the worst of my weaknesses: The first venture capital round led to higher budgets and capital spending, which led to the second venture capital round, which led to higher budgets and capital spending, which led to the third venture capital round. Before I really knew what had happened, my business had grown from twenty-three people in the late summer of 1999 to over 220 in mid-2000.

The fall was sudden and swift. The overburdened vessel of our business was hit by waves from all directions. The stock market began its spiral descent in March 2000, the beginning of a two-year slide that only took seven months to wipe out entirely any venture capital interest in govWorks. At the same time, the results of rushing our product to market and hastily crafting big-business partnerships (with the likes of American Management Systems and Arthur Andersen) began to be felt. The media got wind of a couple of botched client implementations (any entrepreneur who has lived by the sword of positive media coverage will eventually get to know that you die by that sword as well), and our image quickly went from market darling to ugly duckling. Competitors pointed out our weaknesses to prospective customers (one even blast-faxed hundreds of municipal decision makers a negative article that appeared on us in *Fortune Small Business* magazine), and employee morale sank.

As the money dried up, the market soured, and our reputation suffered, I began to cut into our budget and let people go. Even after cutting our staff in half over a period of four months, we were far from profitability, and the effects of multiple layoffs were impossible to avoid: Internet attack sites began prominently featuring my name, filed somewhere between "devil" and "monster." My relationship with my girlfriend fell apart. I could hardly sleep. My board of directors was threatening to resign en masse. A disgruntled former employee threw a rock through my apartment window, and one morning during my commute I discovered—quite dangerously, I might add—that someone had drilled a hole in my car's transmission. In sum, I hit bottom. By December 2000, we had about sixty-five employees, and though profitability was finally in sight, our exorbitant debt levels meant that so was a Chapter 11 bankruptcy filing.

Then, something extraordinary happened. Like the inspiration that kicks off a magical business adventure, it was an epiphany, a moment in time when I suddenly got it. Yet, like the epiphany of many a new business idea, the realization that came to me in December 2000 could be the product only of the grueling experience that preceded it, like the arduous tilling of soil that predates spring's first green sprout. My moment of awakening—of realizing why I was going through everything I was going through and where it was all leading—occurred thousands of miles away from home, during a last-ditch capital-raising trip I had taken to Spain in the waning days of winter. I had gone to see one more venture capitalist, make one last pitch for money to save my business. I was getting so little sleep that by the time I landed in Madrid the morning of the meeting, I was a wreck. I stood in line at immigration, so disoriented I momentarily forgot what country I was entering. The meeting was scheduled for noon in the personal office of the scion of a very well-endowed Spanish family, on a stylish street lined with embassies and shaded by tall, stately oaks. After having been rejected (politely, of course), I stumbled down the elegant stairs of the town house and collapsed in a chair in the entry room. I was so strung out from the stress that I was barely conscious. I closed my eyes. And then, it dawned on me.

I had started my first successful business when I was nineteen years old and put myself through college. I had graduated magna cum laude from Harvard, worked at Goldman Sachs for a number of years, and helped launch a venture capital fund before I was thirty. Until a few short months ago, my second business, govWorks, had been like a rocket ship that would never come back to Earth. I had never experienced professional failure. But there it was, closing in around me, like a brick wall, hard, high, and impenetrable. I was about to experience failure for the first time, broad, raw, and ugly, with nothing to stand in its way. It felt like the end of my world.

Then, a peace stole over me. Almost literally, a door opened in my mind and heart, and through it I was able to see everything that had occurred over the past several years with absolute clarity. I saw how I had gotten caught up in the excitement and the hype of my new business. I saw the way I had begun ignoring my own inner discrimination, the echo of my grandfather telling me to pinch pennies and treat every client as if it were my last. I saw the way I had mishandled and taken for granted relationships that were ultimately more important to me than a business could ever be—relationships with my girlfriend, my business partner, even my own family members. The bright light of these realizations was harsh and difficult to face up to. I had utterly disappointed those employees and investors who had placed their faith in me. It was clear to me in that moment of realization that I was in need of rehabilitation, of "fixing," and that, although many of the lessons I had learned through the govWorks experience were too fresh to have sunk in fully, absorbing them completely over time was going to be the key to a more successful future in business and in my life in general.

I got up from the chair I had collapsed into and stepped outside into the sunlight. The shopkeepers were closing their doors for the siesta, going home to eat with their families. In Madrid, no matter how badly things are going, the siesta always happens. The rhythm of life there is such that nothing is so important it can't wait until after a good meal and a rest. At that moment, I felt like I truly understood this lesson. . . and so many others.

Becoming a Phoenix

The experience I had as govWorks went through its painful tailspin and restructuring (the company was sold to a consortium including First Data Corporation and American Management Systems for less than 10 percent of the value of invested capital in January 2001) was the most difficult experience of my business career *and* the most important. While working at Goldman Sachs, I had occasionally analyzed "distressed" investment opportunities, but I had never been involved directly with a company going through a restructuring. Bringing my own company through the travails of layoffs, product redesigns, balance sheet cleanup—all part and parcel of a corporate restructuring—was a crash course in crisis management. During this painful period, I realized how few professionals (lawyers, accountants, business consultants, or investment bankers) there are who help entrepreneurs and small-business owners navigate crises. After my board of directors resigned, and the cheerleaders of the late '90s dot-com boom (media personalities, investors, hangers-on) had disappeared from sight, I was left alone to deal with concerned clients, employee severance packages, bad PR, and low team morale. "These are the times when you really get to see your true colors," said one of my former board members, a battle-tested West Coast venture capitalist named Mike Levinthal. He was right. I learned a lot more about myself going through the hard times than I did when everything was going great: how to renegotiate vendor debt and office leases, how to communicate openly and honestly with employees in fear of losing their job each day when they come to work, how to keep your client base together when you're trying to make next week's payroll. It was during this hard-luck period of learning that I decided I wanted to share the lessons I was learning with other entrepreneurs. Thus my next business, Recognition Group, was born.

Nearly four years later, Recognition Group has worked with more than fifty companies in various stages of difficult transition—those passing the baton from one generation of leadership to the next, those bringing in outside equity investment capital for the first time, those trying to avoid bankruptcy during a down cycle in the market. Together with the Heart of Entrepreneurship workshops and seminars, Recognition Group allows me to speak directly to the hearts and minds of entrepreneurs and business owners under fire. And I can do so with the kind of experience and empathy that comes only from having been there myself. Even with the most rigorous academic training available in the field of corporate restructuring, I could never work as effectively with entrepreneurs as I do today if I had not lived through my own failure at govWorks.

At Recognition Group, I have brought on partners and consultants who have also been through the wringer of entrepreneurship and are able to speak from their own experience. As a colleague of mine puts it, "You can't expect to help someone avoid the mines unless you've been through the minefield—and even gotten blown up a couple of times." With the benefit of hindsight (Recognition Group has generated more revenues and profits with fewer than fifteen professionals than govWorks ever did, with more than two hundred employees), I can finally say with confidence that everything indeed *does* happen for a reason, and I am *grateful* for my own experience of entrepreneurial failure.

EXERCISE: *Peaks and Valleys*

Becoming grateful for one's own experience(s) of failure is no small feat. But set aside your doubts for a moment. Let yourself be open to learning, open to the possibility of *new* understanding of past experience.

1. Get out your Workbook and a writing utensil, and place them down beside you. Assume your Progress Pose. Slow your breathing. Watch your breath: In. And out. In. And out. If you like, instead of following along in the text, you can listen to this exercise on the audio track for Chapter 5, "Peaks and Valleys," on the *Exercises and Visualizations* CDs.

2. Once you have stilled your posture and your mind, begin to float above your life again, as you did in the Observer exercise of Chapter 3. But this time, don't just float over your workday; let yourself soar at a much higher level—over a period of weeks, years, and months. Go back over your life from today backward and let yourself traverse years at a time, you don't have to dwell on a specific time and place. You don't have to pay the same amount of attention to the last five years as you do to the first five years of your marriage, or your senior versus your sophomore year in college.

3. Let yourself float back and forth over your whole life as if it were a rolling landscape in all directions, the hills being high points of achievement and elation, the valleys being low points of wandering and isolation. View the peaks and valleys with a detached presence of mind, not passing judgment on what you see. You are floating high above the terrain below, and the topography is hardly discernible from this altitude.

4. Swoop lower, so that you are approaching the deepest valley in the landscape. You are approaching the time in your life that was the darkest, the most difficult, the most shrouded and painful. Perhaps you know what it is as you approach it, perhaps you do not. Perhaps it is a divorce, a physical ailment, the shattering of a professional or personal dream. It doesn't have to be something that has a negative association today in your life, or even something you have avoided thinking about. It may be the most basic of life's issues, infusing every day of your existence: You had a child younger than you had planned; you didn't get that graduate degree that you swore you'd complete; you never moved out of the town you grew up in and had always wanted to flee. Let yourself view this valley up close, without getting drawn into the inner dialogue of its drama. Just observe the crisis below, the failure, the disappointment.

5. After you have clearly seen through to the essence of the pain of your deepest valley, raise your eyes and look forward from that experience in your life. Look at how the experience of this valley shaped your life for the *positive*. Look at the decisions and qualities you could never have predicted that came into being as a result of this valley: the beauty and wonder of family life, however unplanned; the resilience and fortitude that came from a health challenge earlier in your life; the empathy for others and aptitude for leadership that came from seeing your company fall apart; your financial situation going from bad to worse at some point.

6. As you look at the good that has come out of your own pain and disappointment, try to see the valleys in the lives of those that are closest to you. We spend so much time caught up in our own head that we rarely consider what others have been through or are going through. Visualize those people who regularly touch your life, and whose lives you touch: your spouse, your children, your parents, your coworkers, your boss, your doctor. See their valleys, too, the most painful and dark moments that they have traversed—or are now traversing—in their lives, and see the world through their eyes for a moment. Your son, who thinks he isn't smart or can't play ball well; your spouse, who battles that chronic back pain; your coworker, who always wanted to be a musician and struggles every day to be happy on the professional path he has chosen. This is empathy: seeing that we all have deep valleys, and our world is affected by the experiences of these valleys, every day, every moment.

7. Now that you have allowed yourself to understand the power and impact of your own deepest valley, and the valleys of those who are close to you, let yourself float again, rising above the landscape once more. See the whole of your life from the serenity of this altitude, the perfect nature of the topography—ups and downs. There is no valley that is meant to be a summit, no summit that is meant to be a valley. The path has its ups and downs, just as it is supposed to. If it didn't it would not have any character to it; it would not be a life.

8. Now open the Workbook to page 137. Record anything and everything that comes to mind with respect to your deepest valley. What did you see? What were you going through at the time? Whom were you going through it with? Perhaps you are going through it right now. As usual, do not censor yourself. It's okay if your thoughts and writing come out in bits and pieces. It may be difficult to write about, or even think about. That's okay too. Write down whatever you can. And free-associate a little, just as you probably did as you were flying in close over your deepest valley. "Bankruptcy," for example, doesn't need to end there. "Fear of losing everything," might be added. Or "humiliation," "confusion," "wondering how to start over." Describe your deepest valley with candor and clear eyes.

9. Turn to page 138 of your Workbook. Record all of your observations of the positive effects that your deepest valley has given (or will give) you in your life. "Caution in entering new relationships," may be one of these gifts, or "gratitude for good health." Don't be confined by what you think you are *supposed* to write. Just record what you saw and felt during the visualization exercise. There is no right or wrong, and the lessons you have learned from your painful experiences in life need not be neat or perfectly logical. One entrepreneur's valley's gift was "being able to distinguish between the real and the bullshit," which she attributed to the fact that a business associate had conned her out of more than $100,000. It's okay if your gifts are nonspecific. "Love" counts, as does "strength" or "patience." Don't rush this exercise. No one else is going to read this Workbook but you, so you can write in sentence fragments, incomplete ideas, or even—as I saw an entrepreneur do once—*draw* the gift(s) your pain or failure has given you.

10. If you want, you also can record the valleys and gifts you observed in those people you interact with daily (a particularly recommended exercise with respect to your spouse or your business partner—people with whom your life is literally in step and whose peaks and valleys may end up being your own!). Beyond the visualization exercise before, in which you observed their experiences from afar, putting their valleys and gifts to writing is likely to deepen your empathy and understanding of their points of view.

Although peaks bestow their own gifts, my emphasis above was on the valleys and not the peaks because it is in the valleys that we learn most of the tough and important life lessons. Although many of us take this to be a self-evident truth when it comes to nonbusiness life (hence religious faith), we tend artificially to separate professional and personal realms, and shy away from studying the valleys—the failures—of our business life. In most of the business world, failure is still a dirty word. Big-company executives in particular talk circles around themselves to avoid saying it. They'd rather say, "Adverse circumstances created a market environment that resulted in sustained negative cash flow," than, "It failed." Yet everybody who has been in business for more than ten minutes—especially anyone who has *run* his or her own business—has experienced a failure of some kind. When I began to talk about my own failure publicly several years ago, and allowed other entrepreneurs to admit to their own valleys and failures, I would feel a sense of relief in the room, as if I was relieving everyone of a dark burden he or she had kept secret. The more accomplished the audience, the greater the sense of relief. But beyond catharsis, openly exploring the valleys in one's life can lead to great realizations of their long-term transformative effect, their gifts. I want to share with you some of the greatest of these gifts that I have heard expressed by entrepreneurs with whom I have performed the Peaks and Valleys visualization.

The Gifts

These gifts capture the recurrent themes that weave themselves through this book—from the currencies and Achilles' heels discussions to the areas of observation and business plan lessons—so it is appropriate that they conclude our lesson plan. Entrepreneurship as a life path is the interjection of the personal with the professional, where your vocation's gifts go far beyond the profitability of your business venture. They are gifts for life.

Alignment

How many times have you heard "timing is everything," when someone tries to describe a relationship that didn't work out, or a business that was started at just the right moment, on the cusp of a consumer trend? Good timing is a form of alignment; it is when our specific actions seem to naturally dovetail with a larger, universal plan. It's the synchronicity we experience when we call an old friend out of the blue, and he happily says, "I was just thinking of you." Or the feeling of being "in the zone," when we decide to make a big personal decision—moving to another city, for example—just as an opportunity arises for employment there or a personal relationship supports the move. Of course, we also know what it's like when our alignment is *off*. We lose our temper at a drop of a dime, not even being able to put our finger on why we're feeling so frustrated. Or we are groggy and slothful in our thinking when trying to win a big new client or make a good impression with a potential source for financing.

In a sense, the entire *Entrepreneur's Success Kit* is about coming into alignment, about getting to know what makes us tick, and making the outer world of our business decisions match up with our inner currencies. Alignment is the fruit of self-contemplation; it is living our entrepreneurial adventure more *consciously*, aware that each outer step forward or backward on the outer level of our business (a breakthrough in our idea, a great new client, or an outburst with an employee) is a manifestation of our inner state of balance, or lack thereof. When *conscious* entrepreneurs reflect on the gifts that have come from their most difficult moments in business or personal life—their valleys—they often identify a new-found respect for and emphasis on balance in their life, *alignment*.

When our mind and heart are in alignment, when our outer ambitions and our inner drives work in concert, we are capable of performing miracles and can withstand any professional crisis. We become more resilient and less fazed by temporary setbacks. Alignment is not a forced discipline, as if you were jamming disparate parts in a machine into place; to the contrary, it is a breathe-easy lightheartedness (some entrepreneurs talk about "keeping things in perspective"—another way of expressing the essence of alignment). A terrifically successful, serial entrepreneur put it to me this way: "I am only as effective as my ability to laugh at myself."

To help you identify when your inner and outer worlds are out of whack, and to learn some practices for how to get back in balance, refer to the track on Chapter 5, "Alignment," on the *Exercises and Visualizations* CDs, as well as Gifts Cards 1 and 2.

The Power of Intention

Intention is the conscious focusing of the will, the decision to do, to create. It is the spark, the genesis, of all entrepreneurial endeavor. Something made you buy this kit. You could have just as easily glanced at the box cover and put it back down, with that maybe-someday expression that most people spend most of their lives making. But you are different. You have the power of intention. You would not have gone this far if you weren't committed to embarking—or hadn't already embarked—on the entrepreneurial path. There is nothing mightier than the human will.

When I lead entrepreneurs through the Peaks and Valleys visualization exercise, unexpected realizations often come up regarding the need for alignment between the outer and inner worlds, the insidious drag of the ego on business relationships, the need to open up and surrender to the rich lessons that life is trying to impart. But no realization is more powerful than the redoubling of will, the conscious awakening to the *power of intention*. When you look back over the valleys in your life, pay special attention to the ascents that followed the low places of pain or disappointment. These climbs began with one difficult step, fortified only by your own determination to get up again. This is your intention, and it is what allows you to scale mountains and turn lemons into lemonade.

Henry Ford, who went bankrupt twice in his first three years in business, said, "Failure is simply the opportunity to begin again, this time more intelligently." Alfred Nobel, one of the nineteenth century's great business tycoons, also experienced two business failures before he was thirty years old. When his factory was destroyed by a nitroglycerine explosion—the death knell of his second business—he is said to have been strangely delighted. His friends and associates thought he was crazy. But it represented just the breakthrough he needed on his way to marketing his greatest invention: dynamite.

Intention is like a wizard's staff: As long as we wield it with conviction, it can perform magic. Every day when you get up, imbue your entrepreneurial project with the power of your intention. Allow your determination and conviction to permeate every aspect of your professional, and personal, life. The tools and exercises in this kit will support you as you make your entrepreneurial intention a reality.

For guidance on how to consciously set—and follow—intentions in your business, refer to the audio track on Chapter 5, "The Power of Intention," on the *Exercises and Visualizations* CDs, as well as Gifts Card 5.

Getting Your Ego Out of It

We've been over this before, even if we haven't named it as directly: Our ego is probably our biggest—and most complex—enemy. It may crop up in the difficulty many of us have in delegating, in our secret belief that we know it all (and hence our proclivity to turn away good advice), or in our tendency to try to wing it when it comes to disciplined financial planning. The metaphor of a double-edged sword is nowhere more appropriate than when applied to the entrepreneurial ego.

On the one hand, our entrepreneurial strivings would never make it past the idea stage if we did not exhibit a healthy self-confidence, and—more grandly—a sense that we were destined to have our own thing and be happy. This is the magic of the entrepreneurial ego, refusing to see ourselves as part of the crowd and inclined to think differently, creatively. On the other hand, that same ego presents the most risk to an enterprise's long-term success once it has gotten off the ground. Having made the leap on our own, we extrapolate that we should do everything without consulting others and, over time, often manage to put off our customers, our partner-collaborators, our vendors, and just about anybody else whom we brush up against with our know-it-all attitude. When entrepreneurs like Robert L. Johnson, Ray Kroc, Martha Stewart, Herb Kelleher, and other strong personalities tell their stories of struggling to get their respective businesses off the ground (or failing at first and starting again), they all stress their need to learn to suppress, manage, and remove the ego from critical decision making. When going through the Peaks and Valleys visualization, entrepreneurs often arrive at the same conclusion: Their most painful experience in business—a busted project, a bankruptcy, a broken partnership—was due to their ego getting in the way of rational decision making.

Pride, stubbornness, and the need to be right have very little place in successful entrepreneurship. Even the most competitive and brazen entrepreneurs you can think of—the Richard Bransons or the Donald Trumps of the world—long ago understood the basic humility of serving a customer. Robert K. Greenleaf popularized the "servant-leadership" model more than thirty years ago, with his ground-breaking essay on the role of the CEO, "The Servant as Leader." It's the old adage: The customer's always right. Getting your ego out of it does not mean being soft or retreating from strong leadership and tough decisions; it means being a leader who can place the pursuit of a world-class product, a satisfied client, or a healthy bottom line above his or her own ego's needs.

To help you identify where your pride may unconsciously be controlling your motivations or actions in your entrepreneurial project, and to look at methods for ego removal, refer to the audio track on Chapter 5, "Getting Your Ego Out of It," on the *Exercises and Visualizations* CDs, as well as Gifts Cards 3 and 4.

Freedom (Trust and Surrender)

The entrepreneurial path is fundamentally spontaneous, unabashed, and daring. The admonitions, guidelines, and "rules" of this kit are like the boundaries on a sporting field; they help you identify what is out-of-bounds and unlikely to be successful, but they should not hinder the free-form beauty of the ball in play. The free flow of creative energy and the unfettered taste for dreaming big and out of the box are essential to successful entrepreneurship. Yet in the midst of this self-possessed freedom, we must learn to trust and surrender to forces greater than us. The valleys we have experienced teach us never to take the freedom and wonder of life for granted.

My deepest valley was actually not the demise of my second business, but a debilitating neck injury I sustained in an accident nearly fifteen years ago. For nearly a year, I was partially paralyzed, and even in the midst of extensive treatment and rehabilitation, the doctors were never sure that the situation would markedly improve. I swore then that I would never take the basics of life— freedom of movement, the ability to work or read without pain—for granted. Although it isn't always easy to keep this feeling of overarching gratitude present and fresh (the neck pain subsided many years ago), I am constantly challenged to do so by my remembrance and the intensity of the original experience. In retrospect, as with the govWorks restructuring, I am grateful for the valley endured through my physical injury. My eventual recovery gave me just enough of a devil-may-care sensibility to dedicate my professional life to entrepreneurship (I figured nothing I encountered on the risky path of entrepreneurship could be nearly as bad as being laid out in physical pain). And the experience of the govWorks bankruptcy gave me the perspective to launch my next entrepreneurial endeavor, capitalizing on the painful knowledge I had gleaned. In both cases, I managed to trust in a higher purpose (not without a lot of kicking and screaming, I have to admit) and ultimately surrender to the lessons life was teaching me.

This act of trust and surrender is one of the hardest things entrepreneurs can do. We carry around a peculiar mix of free and creative energy, often combined with a control-freak nature. These two (seemingly opposite) elements give us the chutzpah to believe we can start our own businesses, attract people to come work for us, convince clients to pay for our services, and perhaps even change the world. The ideas of trust and surrender might clash with our sense of freedom and self-reliance. But true freedom—the freedom that gives us the space to dream and the courage to implement that idea that actually does change the world—comes from knowing that on this entrepreneurial path we will fall and get hurt sometimes and trusting that in this falling there will also be lessons and blessings.

To help you identify where in your entrepreneurial endeavors you are resisting the lessons you are being given, and to help you introduce the magic of trust and surrender into your entrepreneurial experience, refer to the audio track on Chapter 5, "Freedom," on the *Exercises and Visualizations* CDs, as well as Gifts Cards 6 and 7.

Chapter 5 Conclusion

True success comes from enjoying the fullness of the entrepreneurial journey, complete with its incomparable ups and its devastating downs. True success is sucking the marrow out of life and living with no regrets. The ups and downs of the entrepreneurial path are themselves a gift. They invite us to become phoenixes, reinventing ourselves from the ashes of our earlier defeats. The entrepreneurial path is in fact a constant invitation to get to know ourselves better, to aspire to peaks higher than we thought we could reach, and to traverse valleys lower than we thought we could go. It is fundamentally about self-discovery

> *"Work like you don't need the money; dance like no one is watching; love like you have never been hurt."*
> —Irish blessing

and is not for the faint of heart. But there is no professional—or personal—path that is more rewarding, that makes us feel more like our true and full selves. I commend you for walking that path.

The Entrepreneur's Success Kit was designed to support you on your entrepreneurial journey—from practical, personal, and spiritual perspectives. In it, I have shared with you my own experiences and the experiences of other entrepreneurs honestly and openly, so that our collective learning might be of use to you. Still, no amount of written words or audio tracks can ever fully prepare you for the vicissitudes of your individual entrepreneurial journey. You will find your own way: scale your own peaks, plumb your own valleys, and come away with your own entrepreneurial gifts. As you do so, I hope you will reach out and share your experiences with me. You can reach me at kit@kaleil.com or write to me at 40 Broad Street, Suite 500, New York, N.Y. 10004.

Enjoy the journey!